101 Ways to Pay Less Tax

08/09 TAX YEAR

Pat Joseph
Ashley Smith ACCA
Tim Smith FCA CTA
Iain Watson
Hugh Williams FCA

101 Ways to Pay Less Tax
by Pat Joseph, Ashley Smith, Tim Smith, Iain Watson and Hugh Williams

1st edition 2005
2nd edition 2006
3rd edition 2007
    Reprinted 2007
4th edition 2008

© 2008 Lawpack Publishing Limited

Tax regulations are stated as at 14 May 2008, after the emergency Budget.

Lawpack Publishing Limited
76–89 Alscot Road
London SE1 3AW

www.lawpack.co.uk

ISBN: 978-1-905261-82-6

Exclusion of Liability and Disclaimer

Contents

About the authors

Pat Joseph is an Assistant Tax Manager at HM Williams Chartered Accountants; she has extensive experience in tax matters.

Ashley Smith ACCA is an Assistant Tax Manager at HM Williams Chartered Accountants and is a Chartered Certified Accountant.

Tim Smith FCA CTA is Audit and Tax Partner at HM Williams.

Iain Watson is Tax Manager at HM Williams; formerly with HM Revenue & Customs, he offers an invaluable insider's view of tax legislation.

Hugh Williams FCA is Senior Partner at HM Williams, which he founded in 1973; he has written a number of professional books on tax and law.

Representing HM Williams, in 2007 the authors were awarded the 2020 trophy for the most innovative medium-sized UK firm of chartered accountants. In 2002 they were winners of the prestigious Butterworth Tolley Best Small- to Medium-Sized UK Tax Team Award. The firm was also awarded the coveted *Daily Telegraph*/Energis Customer Service Award 2001 in the Professional and Business Services, Small Organisation category.

This book is dedicated to Antony Mills

CHAPTER 1

General principles

1. Put commercial considerations first
2. Working Tax Credits
3. Child Tax Credits
4. Use an accountant
5. Pay tax on time
6. The fundamentals of tax planning
7. Attributes needed by a tax planner
8. How to be a tax planner

Put commercial considerations first

Although this may appear to be the wrong foot on which to start a book about saving tax, you should never put sound commercial judgement after saving tax. In other words, it's nearly always the case that it's better to make money and pay tax than to pay no tax but make no money.

Never let the tax tail wag the common sense dog.

 ## Working Tax Credits

Working Tax Credits are payable whether or not you have children. So if you have no children or only adult children, don't assume that tax credits are not for you; they could be if your income is low enough. You will receive payments directly from HM Revenue & Customs (HMRC).

There are several different parts of the credit, which are paid depending on marital status, the hours worked, your age and whether or not you are disabled. Because of this, there is no 'one size fits all' illustration. However, in most cases where income is below around £15,500 for couples and £11,000 for single people, some credit will be payable if you work 30 hours or more per week. If you are in doubt, it's always best to submit a protective claim (i.e. you can withdraw it later if you subsequently want to) as tax credits are only backdated for three months. This can be done online at www.hmrc.gov.uk or you can contact the tax credit helpline (tel. 0845 300 3900) and ask for a claim form.

 ## Child Tax Credits

As with Working Tax Credits, there are various elements to be taken into account. Generally speaking, you can receive credits if your income is up to £50,000 (£66,000 if the child is under one year). It's worth making a protective claim even if your income slightly exceeds these figures.

Use an accountant

A qualified accountant will know a lot about what your legal obligations are in terms of taxation and will also know lots of ways to legitimately keep your liabilities to a minimum. Generally speaking, your accountant will save you tax better than if you were dealing with matters yourself, and your accountant's fees may be less than the savings you are making. Provided you do as your accountant asks, you also have the peace of mind of knowing that you have complied with your legal obligations.

 ## Pay tax on time

Always pay any tax you owe on time. Interest is charged on late payment at an annualised rate of 7.5 per cent. At current rates, even if you have your money in a high-interest account, it's better to pay HMRC on time. However, if you are going to go overdrawn by paying HMRC, particularly if you don't have an authorised facility, then it's cheaper to pay interest to HMRC than it is to pay interest to your bank.

If your balancing payment (not payments on account) for any given year is paid more than 28 days late, there will be a surcharge of five per cent of the tax still owed at 28 February and a further five per cent will be charged on any sums still not paid by 31 July.

Therefore, if you have to make a balancing payment and a payment on account on 31 January, and you don't have sufficient funds to pay in full, endeavour to settle the balancing payment element by the end of February.

As a general rule, if you owe HMRC money and are unable to pay, you will generally get more favourable treatment by discussing the matter with HMRC's staff rather than burying your head in the sand and avoiding the issue.

 ## The fundamentals of tax planning

All taxpayers have the right to arrange their affairs under the law to minimise their liability to tax. This can be done either by choosing a commercial option which generates a lower tax bill than another, or by organising your financial affairs in such a way so as to minimise the tax bill. While there is nothing wrong with using arrangements set up for no other purpose than to avoid tax, it should be borne in mind that such arrangements may not necessarily be in your wider interest, as we have already said. If you participate in any specialised tax avoidance schemes, a declaration to this effect must be made on your Tax Return.

7 Attributes needed by a tax planner

There are a number of skills required if you are going to plan your tax affairs. These include the following:

1. **The ability to identify a problem:** it may be relatively easy to understand the tax consequences of a problem and even to find a solution. However, the really difficult part is finding out what problems exist in the first place when no-one is there to tell you what they are or even that they exist.

2. **The ability to solve a problem:** even when a problem is identified, not all problems have obvious solutions. Indeed, not all are capable of solution.

3. **Technical knowledge:** don't expect to be a great tax planner if you don't have a sufficiently broad technical knowledge of the subject.

4. **The will to keep your knowledge up to date:** tax is constantly changing. Not only are there annual budgets, Finance Acts and additional legislation to contend with, but also there are Statutory Instruments, case decisions, HMRC concessions and ministerial statements, all of which may affect tax planning.

5. **The ability to interpret legislation:** to the lay person, the Finance Acts appear to be written in a foreign language, so there is a need to master this alien tongue. The answers to most complex tax problems are not to be found in a text book but in the detailed wording of the relevant sections of the legislation.

6. **The ability and tenacity to win an argument:** this is particularly relevant under self-assessment, where HMRC officials may have a

tendency to want to place a different interpretation on a set of facts. You will find that it's necessary to sustain or demolish arguments and bring in new lines of attack to convince the tax authorities of your position.

8 How to be a tax planner

1. The best tax planning accountants think of tax planning every time they open a file. If you are not an accountant, the best way to tax plan is to think about it all the time.

2. Tax planning embraces small as well as large issues. Small changes saving a few hundred pounds of tax a year could well produce as large a saving over a period of time as a major tax-planning exercise. Indeed, while you may be able to save your company £10,000 don't forget to look for a personal saving of £1,000 on your own account at the same time.

3. If your affairs are complex, there may be a greater number of opportunities but the complexity may make them obscure. There may be a tendency for you to forget to look for them but this doesn't mean that they don't exist.

4. Always read the newspapers because there are often good ideas for saving tax contained in the financial pages.

5. Don't nit-pick too much. A saving of £50 may result in more damage to your mental constitution than is merited by a small increase in your personal bank balance.

6. Ask your accountant to try to help you save tax – that's what most people employ accountants for.

CHAPTER 2

For those with low incomes

9. Become a foster carer

10. Claim tax back on any interest you receive

9 Become a foster carer

There is an exemption from tax if you provide foster care to children and young people who are placed with you by local authorities (HSS trusts in Northern Ireland) or independent fostering providers. The first £10,000 plus £200 per week for each child aged under 11 (£250 for over 11s) is tax free. If the amounts you receive exceed these limits, you can choose between paying tax on the excess or on the gross receipts less expenses. This exemption doesn't apply to private fostering arrangements.

If you are an adult placement carer in a scheme recognised by the National Association of Adult Placement Services (NAAPS), there are simplified arrangements for calculating your taxable profit. To qualify, you have to provide accommodation and full-time care for between one and three adults, or respite care. The first option is to claim 'rent-a-room' relief (see number 76). The second option is the fixed-expenses method, whereby you deduct fixed expenses for the adults in your care. These amount to £400 per week for the first adult and £250 for the second and third adults. Any amount you receive over and above this is taxable. However, if the fixed expenses exceed your income, you can't claim loss relief.

Remember, whether you foster an adult or child, you are self-employed and may have to pay National Insurance contributions. However, as explained in number 44, it may be worthwhile paying them.

10 Claim tax back on any interest you receive

Don't pay tax if you don't have to. If your bank or building society is deducting tax from interest and your income is less than:

- £6,035 if you are under the age of 65;
- £9,030 if you are between 65 and 74;
- £9,180 if you are 75 and over;

you should register to receive gross interest. This is quite straightforward. All you have to do is ask your bank/building society for Form R85 and sign it. If the account is in joint names of husband and wife and only one spouse pays tax, the non-tax-paying spouse can receive gross interest on 50 per cent of the interest.

If your income exceeds the above limits by no more than £2,230, you are only liable to pay tax at ten per cent but the bank/building society has to deduct tax at 20 per cent. You can then reclaim the excess by filling in Form R40 (available from your local tax office or on HM Revenue & Customs' website at www.hmrc.gov.uk).

CHAPTER 3

For those with high incomes

11. The Enterprise Investment Scheme (EIS)

12. Venture Capital Trusts (VCTs)

13. Community Investment Tax Relief

14. Maximise pension contributions

15. What income is free from tax?

16. Pension contributions and the over 50s

(11) The Enterprise Investment Scheme (EIS)

Relief from Income Tax and a potential deferral of Capital Gains Tax are both available when a *qualifying individual* subscribes for *eligible shares* in a *qualifying company* carrying on (or intending to carry on) a *qualifying business activity*.

Now, let's look at what this actually means…

A *qualifying individual* is someone who is not connected with the company, which excludes past or present employees and directors, and anyone who controls more than 30 per cent of the capital.

Eligible shares are new ordinary shares which cannot be redeemed for at least three years.

A *qualifying company* is an unquoted trading company, which can include companies quoted on the Alternative Investment Market (AIM) and which carries on its business activity wholly or mainly within the UK. The company must not have plans to become quoted and the assets of the company must not exceed £7 million immediately before the issue of shares or £8 million immediately after the issue of shares.

A *qualifying business activity* is broadly anything that doesn't include, to any substantial extent, the following: accountancy services, legal services, finance, banking, insurance, farming, market gardening, property development, forestry and timber production, leasing, letting, operating or managing hotels, guest houses, nursing and residential care homes.

HM Revenue & Customs (HMRC) will give advance (provisional) approval that the shares will qualify for relief, but that relief will only be due when an EIS3 Certificate has been received from the company.

Investments can be made from the amount of £500 up to a maximum of £500,000 in any tax year. Both husbands and wives have their own limit. If the investment is made before 6 October in a given tax year, up to one half of the amount subscribed for can be carried back to the previous year up to a maximum of £50,000.

Income Tax relief is given at 20 per cent when calculating the investor's tax liability for the year.

If the shares are sold less than three years after they were acquired, then the Income Tax relief is lost. Furthermore, if the investor 'receives value' during the three years, then relief is also lost. There are a number of ways in which an individual can 'receive value' (e.g. by repaying or writing off a debt, making loans or providing other benefits), but this doesn't include the payment of dividends that don't exceed a normal return on investment.

In addition to the Income Tax relief, there are two valuable Capital Gains Tax exemptions. Firstly, provided that the shares have been held for at least three years, when the shares are sold at a profit there is no charge to Capital Gains Tax.

Secondly, if you have a Capital Gains Tax liability, an investment into EIS shares can be used to defer that gain. A claim may be made for any or all of a chargeable gain arising from any source (subject to the annual investment limits) to be invested into EIS shares within one year before and three years after the disposal. The effect of this is that the capital gain on the amount invested is deferred. The deferred gain doesn't become chargeable until the EIS shares are sold or until the investment ceases to be eligible (see conditions above). However, where the hitherto deferred gain becomes chargeable, it can be further deferred by the making of a further EIS investment.

Deferred gains don't become chargeable on the death of the investor.

Venture Capital Trusts (VCTs)

These are, in simple terms, quoted companies that hold EIS-style investments. The investor is still investing in new and expanding companies but not directly, and therefore has less risk.

Tax relief is due when the shares are subscribed for. The maximum investment in any tax year is £200,000. The rate of relief is 30 per cent for 2008/09.

Dividends from ordinary shares in VCTs are exempt from Income Tax provided that shares equal in total to not more than the annual investment limit are acquired in each tax year. The ten per cent tax credit attached to share dividends is still not repayable, but any higher-rate tax liability on the dividends is avoided.

Provided that the shares have been held for at least five years, when the shares are sold at a profit there is no liability to Capital Gains Tax.

VCT investments can, however, no longer be used to defer an existing capital gains liability.

13 Community Investment Tax Relief

The scheme encourages investment in disadvantaged communities by allowing tax relief to individuals and companies which invest through Community Development Finance Institutions (CDFIs). The CDFIs will then invest in businesses and social and community enterprises in under-invested areas. The relief available is 25 per cent of the investment spread over five years (five per cent per year). The investment must be held for a minimum of five years, otherwise the relief may be reduced or withdrawn. There is no upper limit on the amount that can be invested, but there are limits on the amount that can be raised by the CDFIs and that maximum cannot be exceeded.

14 Maximise pension contributions

You get relief at your highest rate of tax for pension contributions. Therefore, if you are a higher-rate taxpayer, it's even more important that you maximise your contributions.

You can get tax relief on contributions up to 100 per cent of your annual earnings (up to an annual allowance set at £235,000). So, if you put £100 into your pension scheme, the tax relief the government gives you on that is worth at least £25.

Even if you are not a taxpayer, you can still get tax relief on pension contributions. You can put in up to £2,880 in any one tax year and the government will top this up with another £720 – giving you total pension savings with tax relief of £3,600 per year.

If your scheme rules allow, you can take up to 25 per cent of your pension fund as a tax-free lump sum.

If your pension pot is more than the 'Lifetime Allowance' when you come to take your pension, you may be subject to a tax charge at that time. But this will only apply if your total pension savings are in excess of £1.65 million from 6 April 2008 (rising to £1.8 million by 2010/11 and reviewed thereafter).

Those individuals with larger pensions pots at A-Day are able to protect their funds from the Lifetime Allowance Charge by completing and submitting the appropriate form to HMRC. They have three years from A-Day to do this.

The rules on when you can take your pension have changed. From 6 April 2010 you won't be able to take a pension before you are 55. There are a couple of exceptions: you will still be able to retire early due to poor health, and if you have the right to retire before 50 at 6 April 2006, that right may be protected.

When contemplating making pension contributions, as with any other investment, it's always important to take good professional advice.

15 What income is free from tax?

- Adoption Allowances
- Adult Placement Carers' Income
- Annuities from gallantry awards
- Attendance Allowance
- Bereavement Payments
- Betting, lottery and pools winnings, and raffle prizes
- Car parking benefits
- Child Benefit
- Child dependency additions
- Child Tax Credit
- Child Trust Funds
- Christmas bonuses paid by the state to pensioners
- Compensation for loss of employment of up to £30,000 (professional advice must be sought)
- Compensation for mis-sold personal pensions
- Council Tax Benefit

- Damages and compensation for personal injury, including interest
- Disability Living Allowance
- Educational Maintenance Allowance
- Foster Care Income
- Gifts for employees from third parties if they are under £250 a year
- Gratuities and bounties from the armed forces
- Guardian's Allowance
- Home improvement, repair and insulation grants
- Housing Benefit
- Incapacity Benefit (short-term – lower rate)
- Incentives for electronic communications
- Income Support
- Individual Savings Accounts (ISAs)
- Industrial injury benefits
- Insurance bond withdrawals of up to five per cent per year (this can be complicated and professional advice should be sought)
- Insurance policy payments (mortgage payment protection, permanent health, etc.)
- Interest from National Savings Certificates
- Interest on overpaid tax
- Interest on Tax Reserve Certificates
- Invalidity pensions
- Jobfinder's Grant
- Jobseeker's Allowance
- Life assurance policy bonuses and profits
- Long-service awards of up to £50 for each year of service (for employees)
- Lump sums from an approved pension scheme
- Luncheon vouchers of up to 15p per day but cash would be taxable – this sum hasn't changed for 40 years!
- Maintenance or alimony payments
- Maternity Allowance
- Miners' Coal Allowance
- National Savings Bank interest of up to £70 per person on ordinary accounts. These accounts are no longer available but the exemption applies to existing account holders
- National Savings Certificates' increase in value
- Pension Credit

- Pensions from Austria or Germany to victims of Nazi persecution
- Personal equity plans (PEPs)
- Premium bond prizes
- Provident benefits paid by a trade union of up to £4,000 for lump-sum payments
- Purchased life annuities – capital element only
- Rent-a-room income up to £4,250 a year
- Save As You Earn Schemes (SAYE) bonuses and interest
- Scholarship income and bursaries
- Severe Disablement Allowances
- Share option profits made under an SAYE option scheme – Capital Gains Tax may be payable
- Shares awarded under an approved Share Incentive Plan (professional advice must be sought)
- Social fund payments
- Statutory Redundancy Pay
- Strike and unemployment pay from a trade union
- Student Grants
- Suggestion scheme awards
- Training allowances for reserve forces
- Travel to work on a works bus
- TV licence payment
- Vaccine damage payment
- Venture Capital Trust dividends
- War Disablement Benefits
- War Widows' Pension
- Winter fuel payments
- Woodlands
- Working Tax Credit

16 Pension contributions and the over 50s

If you are 50 or over, you can make a pension contribution and elect for it to start paying out immediately.

At its best, a higher-rate taxpayer would make a contribution of £3,600 gross, which would equate to a net contribution after 40 per cent tax relief of £2,160, take a lump sum of £900 (25 per cent of the fund value) and the investment would give a gross pension of about £200 per year every year (depending on age, gender, etc.).

This represents a return of over 15 per cent. Even basic-rate taxpayers would have a return of over ten per cent per annum.

From 6 April 2010 you won't be able to take a pension or lump sum before you are 55.

CHAPTER 4
For married couples

17. Equalise your incomes

18. Pay your spouse to work in your business

19. Tax and civil partners

(17) Equalise your incomes

Husbands and wives should always try to equalise their incomes as far as possible so that one spouse is not paying tax at a higher rate than the other. Investments generating interest and dividends can be either moved to joint ownership, or given entirely to the other spouse. Assets that create income (e.g. rented-out land and property) should similarly be put into joint ownership or transferred entirely to the other spouse.

If you are self-employed and your spouse doesn't work, could you employ them in your business? If so, do make sure that you have a contract of employment, that you observe the National Minimum Wage regulations, that what you pay actually changes hands in a demonstrable way and that the pay is commensurate with the services provided.

Alternatively, provided you can show that your spouse plays a significant role in the business you can make them a partner and then the profits can be shared between you.

In other words, where possible, ensure that the spouse with little or no income utilises the personal tax-free allowance, currently £6,035. If the capital is cash on deposit, the interest can be paid gross on completion of Form R85, which is available from banks and building societies.

(18) Pay your spouse to work in your business

Where a spouse works in the family business and payment of wages can be justified, it's generally beneficial to pay at least the equivalent of the lower earnings limit (currently £90 per week) and up to the tax threshold (currently £105 per week). Not only will this be a tax-deductible expense for the employing spouse, but also it will maintain the employee's National Insurance record for state pension purposes. Assuming there is no other income, there will be no tax or National Insurance contributions to pay. Remember, the employer will have to send a P60 (a form which shows gross earnings for the tax year) to HM Revenue & Customs (HMRC) every year so that the National Insurance record can be maintained. Don't forget that you must comply with the minimum wage rates, which are currently

£5.52 per hour, increasing to £5.73 on 1 October 2008. The rate for 18 to 21 year olds is £4.60, increasing to £4.77 on 1 October 2008.

This idea is a useful money saver but you have to do things properly. To make things simpler we are going to imagine that you are a married man running a business, but it could be the other way around or, alternatively, it could involve any business person employing anyone who lives with, or is related to, them and who might reasonably be considered to become an employee.

The way it works is that if you employ your wife for (say) £104 per week, if she has no other earnings or income, she will pay no tax on this pay and you, as her employer, will have reduced your tax bill by more than £1,000. But do watch the following points:

- You need to record the work that she will be doing and the work has to equate to a real contribution to the business. In other words, you cannot just pay her this money without her doing anything in the business at all – the inspector won't allow the payments as a business expense. We include a form (on page 22) that you both might complete and sign as being evidence that she is genuinely working. You simply keep this document to present to the inspector if they ask for it.

- As we have just said, you need to watch out for the minimum wage. You would not be allowed to pay less than that sum, which varies each year.

19 Tax and civil partners

Since 6 December 2005, same-sex couples have been able to register their relationship. From this date, all the tax legislation that applies to married couples also applies to them. For instance, they are able to transfer assets to each other without incurring any Capital Gains Tax. However, if they have two main residences, they can only have one principal private residence exemption, so they may wish to consider making an election to nominate the main residence. They are also able to transfer assets to each other free of Inheritance Tax.

Throughout this book any reference to married couples includes same-sex couples but only with effect from 6 December 2005.

A template form proving that your spouse genuinely works in your company

Agreement between:

_____

and

_____

We, the undersigned, agree that my wife/husband undertakes responsibility for the following activities in my business:

_____

_____

_____

_____

_____

_____

It is agreed that for these services my wife/husband will receive the sum of £_____ per year to be paid monthly.

This arrangement is effective from _____

_____

Signed: _____Proprietor

Signed: _____Wife/Husband

Dated: _____

CHAPTER 5
For employees

20 Claim a flat-rate expense allowance

Certain employees are entitled to a flat-rate expense allowance to cover items such as special clothing, tools, etc. The list below provides details of how much you can claim. You can claim the allowance for the current year and the previous six years.

	£
Agriculture – All workers	100
Aluminium	
Continual casting and process operators	140
De-dimplers	140
Driers	140
Drill punchers	140
Dross unloaders	140
Firefighters	140
Furnace operators and their helpers	140
Leaders	140
Mouldmen	140
Pourers	140
Remelt department labourers	140
Roll flatteners	140
Cable hands	80
Case makers	80
Labourers	80
Mates	80
Truck drivers and measurers	80
Storekeepers	80
Apprentices	60
All other workers	120
Banks – Uniformed employees	60
Brass and copper – All workers	120
Building	
Joiners and carpenters	140
Cement workers	80
Roofing felt	80
Asphalt labourers	80
Labourers and navvies	60
All other workers	120
Building materials	
Stonemasons	120

	£
Tile makers and labourers	60
All other workers	80
Clothing	
Lace makers	60
Hosiery bleachers	60
Dyers	60
Scourers and knitters	60
Knitwear bleachers and dyers	60
All other workers	60
Constructional engineering	
Blacksmiths and their strikers	140
Burners	140
Caulkers	140
Chippers	140
Drillers	140
Erectors	140
Fitters	140
Holders-up	140
Markers off	140
Platers	140
Riggers	140
Riveters	140
Rivet heaters	140
Scaffolders	140
Sheeters	140
Template workers	140
Turners and welders	140
Banksmen labourers	80
Shophelpers	80
Slewers and straighteners	80
Apprentices and storekeepers	60
All other workers	100
Electrical and electricity supply	
Those workers incurring laundry costs only	60
All other workers	120

Engineering

Pattern makers	140
Labourers, supervisory and unskilled workers	80
Apprentices and storekeepers	60
Motor mechanics in garage repair shops	120
All other workers	120

Fire service

Uniformed firefighters and fire officers	80

Food – All workers | 60

Forestry – All workers | 100

Glass – All workers | 80

Healthcare

Ambulance staff on active service	140
Nurses	100
Midwives	100
Chiropodists	100
Dental nurses	100
Occupational, speech and other therapists	100
Phlebotomists	100
Physiotherapists	100
Radiographers	100
Plaster room orderlies	100
Hospital porters	100
Ward clerks	100
Sterile supply workers	100
Hospital domestics	100
Hospital catering staff	100
Laboratory staff	60
Pharmacists	60
Pharmacy assistants	60
Uniformed ancillary staff	60

Heating

Pipe fitters and plumbers	120
Coverers	120
Laggers	120
Domestic glaziers	120
Heating engineers and their mates	120
All other workers	100

Iron and steel | 80

Day labourers	80
General labourers	80
Stockmen	80
Timekeepers	80
Warehouse staff	80
Weighmen	80
Apprentices	60
All other workers	140

Iron mining

Fillers	120
Miners	120
Underground workers	120
All other workers	100

Leather

Curriers (wet workers)	80
Fellmongering workers	80
Tanning operatives (wet)	80
All other workers	60

Particular engineering

Pattern makers	140
Chainmakers	120
Cleaners	120
Galvanisers	120
Tinners	120
Wire drawers in the wire drawing industry	120
Toolmakers in the lock-making industry	120
Apprentices and storekeepers	60
All other workers	80

Police force

Police officers (ranks up to and including Chief Inspector)	140
Police community safety officers	140

Precious metals – All workers | 100

Printing – Letter press section using rotary presses

Electrical engineers	140
Electro-typers	140
Ink and roller markers	140
Machine minders	140
Maintenance engineers	140
Stereotypers	140
Benchhands	60
Compositors	60

Readers	60	Riveters	140
T & E section	60	Sheet ironworkers	140
Wireroom operators	60	Shipwrights	140
Warehousemen	60	Tubers	140
All other workers	100	Welders	140
Prisons		Labourers	80
Uniformed prison officers	80	Apprentices and storekeepers	60
(Don't forget to claim for the		All other workers	100
costs of keeping your dog)		**Textiles and textile printing**	
Public service		Carders	120
Dock and inland waterways:		Carding engineers	120
Dockers	80	Overlookers	120
Dredger drivers	80	Technicians in spinning mills	120
Hopper steerers	80	All other workers	80
All other workers	60	**Vehicles**	
Public transport:		Builders	140
Garage hands including cleaners	80	Railway vehicle repairers	140
Conductors and drivers	60	Railway wagon lifters	140
Quarrying		Railway vehicle painters and	
All workers	100	letterers	80
Railways		Railway wagon, etc. builders' and	
All workers except craftsmen	100	repairers' assistants	80
(For craftsmen, see appropriate		All other workers	60
industry)		**Wood and furniture**	
Seamen		Carpenters	140
Carpenters (passenger liners)	165	Cabinet makers	140
Carpenters (cargo vessels,		Joiners	140
tankers, coasters and ferries)	140	Wood carvers	140
Shipyards		Wood cutting machinists	140
Blacksmiths and their strikers	140	Artificial limb makers	
Boilermakers	140	(other than in wood)	120
Burners	140	Organ builders	120
Carpenters	140	Packaging case makers	120
Caulkers	140	Coopers not providing own tools	60
Drillers	140	Labourers	60
Furnacemen	140	Polishers	60
Holders-up	140	Upholsterers	60
Fitters	140	All other workers	100
Platers	140		
Plumbers	140		

HM Revenue & Customs' (HMRC) website (www.hmrc.gov.uk/manuals/
eimanual/index.htm) at EIM 50000 to EIM 70199 contains a lot of

information about particular occupations and the expenses that can be claimed for them. For example, nursing staff (which includes midwives of all grades, auxiliaries, students and assistants) can claim £100 per annum laundry allowance, £12 per annum shoe allowance and £6 per annum stocking allowance. (For male nurses this can include socks.)

We therefore strongly recommend everyone having a look at this part of the website to ensure that they are claiming their due.

You claim under Box 18 on the employment pages of the Tax Return.

 ## Professional subscriptions

If you are an employee and you pay professional subscriptions and:

- you are required to do so as a condition of your employment; or
- the activities of the body are directly relevant to your employment;

then provided the professional body is referred to in List 3 (which can be found on HMRC's website at www.hmrc.gov.uk/list3/index.htm), you can claim tax relief for the subscription.

You claim under Box 19 on the employment pages of the Tax Return.

 ## Claim incidental expenses when travelling on business

If you are an employee and you have to travel as part of your job, you can claim for your travel costs. This doesn't include ordinary commuting from home to your normal place of work. However, if you work on a site, i.e. you don't have a normal fixed place of work, you can claim the cost of home to site travel provided the duration of your work at the specific site doesn't exceed 24 months.

Incidental personal expenses for items such as newspapers, personal phone calls and laundry incurred while away overnight on business trips are tax free providing the employer pays or reimburses no more than £5 per night for UK trips and £10 for overseas trips. If these limits are exceeded, the whole amount is taxable.

The full cost of meals and accommodation while travelling or staying away on business is also an allowable expense.

You claim under Box 17 on the employment pages of the Tax Return.

Rather than claiming actual travelling costs, if you use your own car for business travel, you can claim for business mileage – see number 36 for more information.

23 Claim expenses against your employment income

If you incur extra costs as an employee, keep a record of the details and dates on which the expenditure was incurred, together with the bills, and you may be able to claim it on your Tax Return – see Box 20 on the employment pages of the Tax Return.

Here are some items that you might be able to claim for, unless they are covered by one of HMRC's fixed-rate allowances (see number 20) (i.e. you cannot claim more than once):

- Overalls
- Boots
- Helmets
- Gloves
- Protective clothing
- Necessary equipment
- Tool bag
- Tools
- Trade journals and technical books
- Part of your own telephone bill covering calls to customers
- Gifts to customers paid for by yourself which don't cost more than £50

- Fees or subscriptions to an organisation (professional or otherwise) of which you are a member, although HMRC must approve the organisation

- Journals and publications, etc.

If you have to borrow money to buy equipment that is necessary for your job, then the interest can be claimed as an expense. This doesn't extend to car loans nor to a bank overdraft or credit card interest.

The general rule is that all such expenses must be incurred wholly, exclusively and necessarily for the purposes of the employment.

Elsewhere in this book (see number 20) we cover the fixed allowances you may be able to claim. As we say elsewhere, please note that a number of categories of workers, including healthcare workers, have fixed-rate expenses that they can claim. You may even be able to claim back for earlier years that you haven't already claimed for.

You claim under Box 20 on the employment pages of the Tax Return.

24 Claim for the use of your home as an office

If you are required to work at home and use a specific room for this purpose, you can claim an allowance based on a proportion of the total upkeep. You claim under Box 20 on the employment pages of the Tax Return.

Alternatively, you can claim the £2 per week to cover the additional costs of working at home. This is obviously a small figure but doesn't need to be supported by documentary evidence.

25 Submit your Tax Return on time

If you are an employee and have been issued with a Tax Return, submit the completed form to HMRC by 30 September. Not only will HMRC calculate your tax liability for you, but if you do owe any tax, it will include it in next year's tax code provided your employment is continuing.

If an underpayment is included in your tax code, and the amount of extra tax you are paying is causing you hardship, ask HMRC to spread the payment over two or three years.

Join the company pension scheme

If your employer offers access to a pension scheme, it's almost certainly a good thing to do.

When losing your job

If you lose your job, you may be entitled to a tax-free lump sum of up to £30,000. This will apply if you have been made redundant because your job no longer exists. If you are allowed to keep your company car as part of your redundancy package, the market value of the car will be taken into account in calculating the £30,000. Payments in excess of this amount will be taxable as well as payments made in recognition of past services.

Most other lump-sum/ex gratia payments will be taxable unless made as compensation for the company breaching your contract of employment.

However, if your contract of employment gives you a right to compensation when your employment ends, then the lump sum will be taxable regardless of the amount.

Statutory redundancy payments are not taxable but they do count towards the £30,000 limit.

Would you pay less tax if you went self-employed?

The answer is almost certainly 'yes' because there are many more expenses that you can claim. However, if you are going to go self-employed, you have to do so properly or HMRC will catch up with you and either you or your deemed employer will suffer the tax. On top of this there will also be backdated National Insurance to pay, interest on the late payments and, on top of that, the taxman will demand a penalty. So do make sure that you get it right.

To help you find out whether HMRC is likely to accept that you are truly self-employed, here is a set of questions that should give you an idea:

1. Is there a contract of service, i.e. a contract of employment?

    A 'no' answer indicates self-employment.

2. Is there a contract for services, i.e. a notice supplied by the person carrying out the work (A), indicating the nature of goods or services they will provide to B (this need not be written)?

    A 'yes' answer indicates self-employment.

3. Is the person who does the work in business on their own account?

    A 'yes' answer indicates self-employment.

4. If the person is in business on their own account, has evidence been provided that this is indeed the case (e.g. copy accounts, the payment of Class 2 National Insurance contributions)?

    A 'yes' answer indicates self-employment.

5. Are the hours worked decided by the person doing the work?

    A 'yes' answer indicates self-employment.

6. Are the days worked decided by the person doing the work?

    A 'yes' answer indicates self-employment.

7. Does the person doing the work decide when to take their own holidays?

    A 'yes' answer indicates self-employment.

8. Does the business proprietor supervise the work?

    A 'no' answer indicates self-employment.

9. Is the person part and parcel of the business?

    A 'no' answer indicates self-employment.

10. Does the person supply tools and/or materials when they carry out the work?

    A 'yes' answer indicates self-employment.

11. Does the person doing the work give the business an invoice for the work done?

    A 'yes' answer indicates self-employment.

12. Does the business calculate how much to pay the person doing the work and give a payslip?

    A 'no' answer indicates self-employment.

13. Is self-employment the intention of both parties?

    A 'yes' answer indicates self-employment.

14. Is the person bound by the customer care credo of the business?

    A 'no' answer indicates self-employment.

15. Is the person carrying out the work required to wear a uniform or dress tidily at the diktat of the business?

    A 'no' answer indicates self-employment.

16. Is the person carrying out the work provided with a car or transport by the business?

    A 'no' answer indicates self-employment.

17. In the event of sickness, does the business continue to pay the person while not at work?

    A 'no' answer indicates self-employment.

18. Is the person carrying out the work at liberty to work for other businesses?

    A 'yes' answer indicates self-employment.

19. Is the person carrying out the work required to work in order to perform a specific task?

    A 'yes' answer indicates self-employment.

20. Does the business, on asking this person to carry out work for it, assume any responsibility or liability characteristic of an employment, such as employment protection, employees' liability, pension entitlements, etc.?

    A 'no' answer indicates self-employment.

21. Is the person who does the work paid an agreed price per job?

A 'yes' answer indicates self-employment (i.e. they are not paid for the hours they work but for the work carried out).

22. Is the work carried out regularly?

A 'no' answer indicates self-employment.

23. Does the individual work for other people?

A 'yes' answer indicates self-employment.

24. Does the person carrying out the work advertise?

A 'yes' answer indicates self-employment.

25. Does the person carrying out the work have headed stationery?

A 'yes' answer indicates self-employment.

26. Can the person send a substitute? If so, has this ever happened?

A 'yes' answer indicates self-employment.

27. Does the person have to rectify faulty workmanship in their own time and at their own expense?

A 'yes' answer indicates self-employment.

29 Moving because of your job?

If you are moving home because of your job, qualifying removal expenses and benefits are exempt from Income Tax. The maximum tax-free amount is £8,000 per move provided that expenses and benefits are incurred in the period from the date of the job change up to the end of the tax year following the one in which the move occurred.

This applies whether it's a new job with a new employer, a new job with an existing employer or you are continuing your current job but at a new location. Issues of ease of daily travelling from the old and new homes have to be regarded and the expenses have to be reimbursed by your employer. Most of the costs reasonably related to the move, subject to limits, are allowed and full details are in HMRC's booklet *IR134*.

The favourable tax and National Insurance contributions treatment of these payments should make them attractive to employee and employer alike when considering relocation packages.

CHAPTER 6
For employers

30. Short-term employment contracts

31. Share schemes

32. File your PAYE Return online

33. Tax-free benefits you can give to employees

Short-term employment contracts

If you are an employer, particularly where your business's workload varies significantly throughout the year, do consider having your employees on short-term contracts. This gives you flexibility if you need to reduce the number of staff and avoids you having to make redundancy payments. You are still at liberty to give fresh contracts to those people whose services you wish to retain.

 ## Share schemes

Offer your employees shares under one of the many share schemes available. This can be a tax-efficient way of passing a valuable benefit to an employee.

What are the rules if I provide shares and share options for my employees?

A Share Incentive Plan (SIP) is a plan established by a company and approved by HM Revenue & Customs. Employees may allocate part of their salary to shares in the company ('partnership shares') without paying tax or National Insurance contributions, nor are employers' National Insurance contributions payable. Employers may also give free shares to employees, including extra free shares for employees who have partnership shares ('matching shares'), and the cost of the shares and of running the scheme are tax-deductible. The maximum you can allocate as an employer is £1,500 per year for partnership shares and £3,000 worth of free shares per year, although employers may set lower limits. Note: all types of share issued to employees must be reported to HM Revenue & Customs (HMRC) on Form 42 within 30 days; failure to so do will entail a fine of £300 per employee.

If the employee takes shares out of the scheme within five years, there will be a tax charge. If the shares remain in the scheme for five years or more, they are free of tax and National Insurance contributions when they are withdrawn.

There are two types of share option scheme: 'Save As You Earn' (SAYE) – linked share option schemes – and Company Share Option Plans. Under an SAYE scheme, contributions of between £5 and £250 per month are paid by the employee under a SAYE contract with a building society or bank. The option to purchase shares using the SAYE funds can normally be exercised after three, five or seven years when the contract ends. No charge to Income Tax arises on the difference between cost and market value when a share option is exercised, nor at the time that it's granted.

The scheme enables an option to be granted now to acquire shares at today's price. The price at which the option may be exercised must not normally be less than 80 per cent of the market value of the shares at the time the option is granted.

Under Company Share Option Plans, the option must not be granted at a discount and the total market value of shares that may be acquired under the option must not exceed £30,000. If these conditions are complied with, there is no tax charge when options are granted. Nor is there a tax charge when the option is exercised, providing options under the scheme are exercised between three and ten years after they are granted, and not more frequently than once in three years.

The costs of running the scheme are tax-deductible.

What are the different schemes for providing shares for employees?

The different schemes are:

- Share Incentive Plans (SIP): Under this scheme, which is also known as an AESOP (All Employee Share Ownership Plan):
  - employers can give up to £3,000 worth of shares to each employee;
  - employees can buy up to £1,500 worth of shares and, under such circumstances, employers can reward the purchasers with two free shares for each share purchased.
- SAYE Option Schemes:
  - Participants can save up to £250 per month to acquire shares at the end of a three-, five- or seven-year period.

- Enterprise Management Incentive (EMI):

  - Companies with gross assets not exceeding £30 million can grant tax and National Insurance contribution-advantaged share options worth up to £100,000 to any number of employees, subject to a total value of £3 million.

- Company Share Option Plans (CSOP):

  - Up to £30,000 of options each can be granted to any number of employees with tax and National Insurance contribution advantages.

- Schemes outside HMRC approved range of schemes:

  - These will suffer tax and National Insurance contributions.

Needless to say, professional advice must be sought.

File your PAYE Return online

Small employers (those with fewer than 50 employees) qualify for a tax-free payment if they file their end of year PAYE Returns online. The incentive is being paid as follows:

- 2007/08 – £100
- 2008/09 – £75

The Returns must be completed correctly, filed electronically on time and must meet quality standards. Employers who operate PAYE manually should consider switching.

33 Tax-free benefits you can give to employees

Give your employees tax-free benefits, such as:

- a canteen if it's available to everybody;
- car and bike parking at work;

- childcare costs and vouchers – not taxable up to £55 per week;
- computers provided solely for business use, and any private use is not significant, are exempt from a benefit charge;
- exam prizes – they are not taxable if they are reasonable and not part of the employment contract;
- mileage allowances (up to 40p per mile for the first 10,000 miles and 25p per mile after that);
- mobile telephones;
- nurseries and play schemes run by the employer;
- outplacement counselling;
- pension contributions and death-in-service cover;
- relocation expenses – tax free up to £8,000;
- retraining and counselling on leaving employment;
- share incentive schemes – not taxable if approved by HMRC;
- travel to work on a works' bus;
- workplace sports facilities;
- suggestion scheme awards;
- medical check-ups for employees and their families;
- bicycles provided for employees as long as they are used for travel between home and work and private use is limited (this includes bicycle safety equipment);
- Christmas parties open to all staff. You can now spend up to £150 per head. It will be a tax deductible business expense and tax free for your employees.

The benefit to the employer is that the employees get a good deal, while the employer gets tax relief on the expenditure incurred.

CHAPTER 7

Company cars

34. Vans have some tax-saving attractions

35. Company cars

36. Claim approved mileage allowance payments for your car

37. Avoid the fuel tax charge

38. Own your own car rather than using your employer's

Vans have some tax-saving attractions

If you are an employee, are provided with a company van and make private use of it, you pay tax on a standard benefit (if benefit it be) of £3,000 per year, regardless of the age of the van. If the van is shared, then the taxable benefit is spread between the sharers.

However, if you use your company van for restricted private purposes, there is no tax to pay. You can use it for going to and from work but most other private uses would create a charge. Examples of other uses that create a tax charge, according to HM Revenue & Customs (HMRC), are:

- using the van to visit the supermarket twice a week;
- taking it on holiday;
- using it for social activities.

But uses that don't trigger a tax charge include:

- taking rubbish to the tip once or twice a year;
- regularly taking a detour to the newsagent on the way to work;
- calling at the dentist on the way home.

There is also a fuel benefit charge of £500. This doesn't apply if the fuel is made available for business travel only or the employee is required to pay for the fuel used for private purposes and does, in fact, do so.

35 Company cars

The company car tax charge is calculated by referring to the list price of the car when new, plus any additional items fitted and less any capital contributions made by the employee, and the CO_2 emissions (which are shown on the V5 vehicle registration document) for cars registered on or after 1 March 2001 (see the table opposite). Emission levels can also be found on the internet at the Vehicle Certification Agency's website (www.vca.gov.uk) and that of the Society of Motor Manufacturers and Traders Limited (www.smmt.co.uk).

Car benefit charges based on CO₂ emissions

CO₂ emissions in grams per kilometre		Tax is based on the following percentage of the price of the car
2008–2009	2007–2008	%
120		10*
135	140	15*
140	145	16*
145	150	17*
150	155	18*
155	160	19*
160	165	20*
165	170	21*
170	175	22*
175	180	23*
180	185	24*
185	190	25*
190	195	26*
195	200	27*
200	205	28*
205	210	29*
210	215	30*
215	220	31*
220	225	32*
225	230	33**
230	235	34***
235	240	35****

*	add 3% if car runs solely on diesel
**	add 2% if car runs solely on diesel
***	add 1% if car runs solely on diesel
****	maximum charge so no supplement
Note:	The exact CO₂ figure is rounded down to the nearest five grams per kilometre (gm/km).

Diesel cars are subject to a three per cent surcharge unless they meet Euro 4 standards (up to 6 April 2006). From 6 April 2006, the surcharge no longer applies to all Euro 4 standard diesels registered after 1 January 2006. The three per cent reduction, however, continues to apply to all Euro 4 diesels registered before 1 January 2006 for the rest of their life. See the HMRC's website for further details.

If a vehicle isn't available for the full year, then the charge is reduced pro-rata.

Therefore, selecting a car with lower emissions and/or a lower list price will reduce your tax liability.

If you are self-employed and are going to use a car for business purposes, you can claim enhanced capital allowances (see page 52) if your new car has emissions not exceeding 110 gm/km. You will be able to claim 100 per cent first-year allowances (subject to an adjustment for any private use).

Don't forget that the level of road tax you have to pay is also reduced for lower-emission cars. See the table below.

£ per Year VED Band	CO2 (g/km)	Petrol & Diesel Cars
Graduated Vehicle Excise Duty for Private Vehicles (Registered from March 2001)		
A	100 and below	£0
B	101 to 120	£35
C	121 to 150	£120
D	151 to 165	£145
E	166 to 185	£170
F	186 to 225	£210
G*	226 and above	£400

* For new cars registered on or after 23 March 2006

36 Claim approved mileage allowance payments for your car

If you are an employee and you use your own car for business purposes, you can claim back 40p per mile from your employer for the first 10,000 business miles in a tax year and 25p per mile thereafter. If your employer reimburses less than the mileage figure, you can claim the difference in your Tax Return (Box 17 on the employment pages). If you can persuade your employer to pay you an extra 5p per mile for carrying a business passenger, it would also be tax free, but you can't claim it if your employer doesn't pay you for it. If you use a motorbike, you can claim 24p for business mileage and if you use a bicycle, you can claim 20p.

Avoid the fuel tax charge

If your employer pays for all your fuel but you repay him for all your private fuel and if you keep a careful and detailed record of every car journey undertaken whether business or private, then you don't have to pay tax on the fuel provided for business purposes. However, you have to bear in mind that travel from home to the place of work is considered to be private mileage.

The company car fuel multiplier is £16,900. You multiply this by the appropriate percentage taken from the table on page 43 to work out the taxable benefit for your car.

 ## Own your own car rather than using your employer's

The tax payable on car benefits is now so high that it can often be cheaper to own your own car and use it for your employer's business. You would need to work it out and we certainly know of cases where, while the tax is high, the employee would rather suffer the tax than have to pay for all the outgoings that having one's own car entails. However, as we say, with the tax being high, it's quite likely that you would be better off if you owned your own car than paid the taxes that driving an employer's business car attracts.

CHAPTER 8

For those running their own business

39. Travelling expenses

40. Limited companies

41. Introduce goodwill to create a large director's loan account and pay very little tax

42. Don't automatically reclaim VAT on fuel

43. The flat-rate VAT scheme

44. National Insurance

45. Annual Investment Allowance and First-Year Allowances

46. The tax advantages of converting commercial property into residential use

47. The benefit of short-life assets

48. Use your business's losses

49. Have you claimed for all your business expenses?

50. Farmers and averaging

51. Partnerships

52. Claiming tax relief on interest

39 Travelling expenses

Expenses	Employer	Self-employed	Can VAT (input tax) be reclaimed?
	Where expenses are incurred by the employer, whether a self-employed trader, a partnership or a company	Where a self-employed trader incurs these expenses on his own behalf	
Entertaining own staff	Allowable	Allowable	Yes*
Business travel between place of business and customers, etc. (but not home)	Allowable	Allowable	Yes
Hotel bills, etc.	Allowable	Allowable	Yes, so long as it's billed to the VAT registered trader
Drinks and meals away from home:			
1. Working/selling	Allowable	Not allowable	Yes*
2. On training course	Allowable	Allowable	Yes*
3. Buying, etc. trips	Allowable	Allowable	Yes*
Entertaining business clients:	Not allowable	Not allowable	No
Car parking	Allowable	Allowable	Yes
Trade show expenses	Allowable	Allowable	Yes
Petrol	Allowable	Allowable – business proportion only	Yes**

* But not if there is any measurable degree of business entertainment.

** But if the input VAT is reclaimed, remember to include the scale charge in your output tax on the VAT Return.

40 Limited companies

As a private individual, your highest rate of Income Tax is 40 per cent and that starts when your taxable income reaches £34,800. On top of the Income Tax bill, there is Class 4 National Insurance to add to it.

However, for a company the highest rate of Corporation Tax is 28 per cent and that only starts when its taxable profits are over £1.5m. The rate below that is 21 per cent. The marginal rate between £300,000 and £1.5m is 29.75 per cent.

If you and your spouse have a business and the taxable profits are £100,000, if we ignore personal allowances, here is how the sums work out:

Self-employment/Partnership				Tax, etc. payable
Profits				
£100,000				
		Husband	*Wife*	
Profits Shared		£50,000	£50,000	
Income Tax				
34,800	20%	6,960	6,960	
15,200	40%	6,080	6,080	
50,000		13,040	13,040	26,080
Class 4 National Insurance				
5,435	0%	0	0	
34,605	8%	2,768	2,768	
9,960	1%	100	100	
50,000		2,868	2,868	5,736
Total tax and National Insurance payable				£31,816
The money the Chancellor allows you to keep				**£68,184** 68%
Company Profits	Corporation Tax			
£100,000	21%			21,000
The money the Chancellor allows the company to keep				**£79,000** 79%

In other words, the tax saved by trading through a limited company appears to be over £10,000.

However, it's not quite as simple as that (it never is!) because if you have paid yourself a salary from the company, then you may have suffered the higher personal rates of tax, and the company and you will both have suffered National Insurance contributions. On the other hand and in addition, you may have paid yourself a dividend, which can be a very tax efficient way of getting paid. You can also control the amount of income you receive to avoid higher rate tax.

So it's all quite complicated and professional advice must be sought. But if these figures relate in any way to what you are doing, you should discuss this with your accountant – there could be a large tax saving to be made.

41 Introduce goodwill to create a large director's loan account and pay very little tax

This should not be entered into lightly nor without professional help, but, with careful planning, if you incorporate an existing business (i.e. turn it into a limited company), you should be able to create a sum for goodwill. We don't want to confuse you with science here, but, if you introduce a sum for goodwill from your present business as you incorporate, as the business proprietor you will have created a sum in the company's balance sheet – a sum that is due back to you.

It may make more sense if we give you an example:

Let's say you have a business and it's making profits of £40,000. Now you could follow the general rule and say that a business is worth three times its profits – so this might make your business worth £120,000. But there may already be assets in your business worth £90,000, which could be cash, buildings, equipment, etc. If they are already in the business, then it would not be unreasonable to say that the value of goodwill in your business is £30,000 (i.e. the difference between what the business is worth and the assets already in it).

So you put a value of £30,000 on goodwill and the company now owes you £30,000 for this goodwill. You are then in a position to draw £30,000 out of your business tax free – when the cash-flow allows you.

One thing to beware of is that you may be liable for Capital Gains Tax for handing a valuable sum for goodwill to a company.

As we say, you will need professional advice over this, particularly because goodwill valuation is complicated, but it's a very useful way of drawing tax-free cash from a business.

42 Don't automatically reclaim VAT on fuel

It's not always a good idea to claim input tax (i.e. the VAT you have to pay) on fuel.

The rule over claiming input tax on your fuel purchases is that if you claim VAT on your fuel purchases and some of the fuel is used for private journeys, you have to add the fuel scale charge to your output tax (i.e. the VAT you charge your customers) – you will find the figures for the quarterly fuel scale charge in the Appendix. What this can mean (and is the usual case) is that you can end up paying HM Revenue & Customs (HMRC) more than you are claiming back from it and this may not easily be worth your while. The only person who can work out whether it's worth your while is you. Since 1 May 2007 the fuel scale charge is based on the CO_2 rating of the car.

 ## The flat-rate VAT scheme

Are you registered for VAT but hate the complexity of VAT returns? Provided your turnover is less than £150,000 per annum, then it's possible to request that the flat-rate scheme applies. The payment due to Customs and Excise is a percentage of your standard-rated turnover, so you don't have to calculate your input VAT every quarter. The exact percentage applied is determined by the nature of your business activity and full details are available on the Customs and Excise website. Switching to this scheme could save you time and money, but you would have to look at each case on its own merits. If you usually have a large amount of input VAT, then the scheme may not be suitable for you.

 ## National Insurance

While most of the ideas for reducing your tax bill in this book involve larger sums of tax saving, this one concerns one of the smallest figures of savings on offer, if not the smallest.

If you are just starting out in business, you are unlikely to make large profits in your first year of trading. This is not guaranteed to happen but it usually turns out this way.

Now you have to register your business with HMRC and they will demand that, as a self-employed person, you pay Class 2 National Insurance contributions of £2.30 per week. Such a sum is unlikely to break the bank but you can get into trouble if you don't pay it.

However, if your profits are to be under £4,825 (2008/09 figure), you can claim exemption from paying it. Do remember that opting out may affect your entitlement to state pension, Statutory Maternity Pay, Incapacity Benefit, Bereavement Allowance and other contributory benefits. The current rate is only £2.30 per week, which we think is a small price to pay for maintaining your National Insurance record.

45 Annual Investment Allowance and First-Year Allowances

Annual Investment Allowance: This is a new allowance applicable from April 2008. Expenditure of up to £50,000 per annum on plant, machinery, long life assets and integral features will be relieved in full against profits. Any expenditure above this limit will be relieved using the normal capital allowance rules. Where an accounting period spans 1 April for companies, or 6 April for individuals, this allowance is reduced pro rata. Similarly, accounting periods which are less than, or greater than, 12 months will also get a reduced allowance.

From 1 April 2008 (for companies) or 6 April 2008 (for individuals), where the written down value of the plant and machinery pool is £1,000 or less, this can be written off in full if desired. These two changes taken together mean that many small businesses – especially those which are labour rather than capital intensive, as are many service businesses – will be able to claim 100 per cent of their capital expenditure in the year in which they make it. This is a useful and worthwhile simplification.

Long life assets: Long life assets are items of plant or machinery which are expected to last at least 25 years. The writing down allowance for them is increased from six per cent to ten per cent. A new 'pool' is created to include long life assets and integral features.

As a consequence of the changes in the rates applicable to the different pools, a 'hybrid rate' of capital allowances has to be calculated when the accounting period spans 1 April (companies) or 6 April (individuals). For example, with an accounting period covering 1 January 2008 to 31 December 2008, the hybrid rate of capital allowances would be:

91/366 x 25%	=	6.22%
275/366 x 20%	=	15.03%
Hybrid rate for the transitional period	=	21.25%

First-Year Allowances: A business can claim 100 per cent First-Year Allowances (i.e. you can effectively write off all the capital costs against your trading profit) if it incurs qualifying expenditure on designated energy-saving or water-saving plant and machinery. There are currently 28 categories in all, including such things as lighting, heating, refrigeration, flushes, taps, leakage detection equipment and flow control equipment.

If you are considering purchasing plant or equipment that is in the specified categories, then to buy the energy efficient option will (a) give you full tax relief immediately, (b) probably reduce your long-term running costs and (c) help save the planet.

Before spending your money, visit the Enhanced Capital Allowances website at www.eca.gov.uk. This list is constantly being updated so do check it regularly.

Small businesses can still claim First-Year Allowances of 50 per cent on all plant and equipment purchased in 2008/09, but it will usually be best to claim relief under the new Annual Investment Allowance rules covering expenditure up to £50,000. The rate of relief for medium-sized businesses remains unchanged at 40 per cent. (A medium-sized business is one with a turnover of less than £22.8 million and less than 250 employees.)

Other capital allowances: Agricultural buildings allowances and industrial buildings allowances are being phased out over a four-year period. But the allowances can still be claimed on new expenditure during the phase out period but at a reduced rate. Furthermore, there is no tax charge or tax relief on the sale of the building after 21 March 2007, unless there was a contract for sale at that date.

46 The tax advantages of converting commercial property into residential use

If you have a shop or other commercial premises with vacant or underused premises above, capital allowances can be claimed on converting this space into residential flats. The capital allowances are treated as expenditure when calculating the letting profit or loss. An initial allowance of 100 per cent is available if desired. While there may be a balancing adjustment needed if the property is sold within seven years of the flat being available to let, there is no adjustment for disposals after that time.

To qualify, the properties must have been built before 1980, the ground floor must be rated for business use, there must be no more than four upper storeys, they must have been empty or used for storage for at least a year and the new development must not have more than four rooms, excluding bathroom and kitchen. There are also income limits in respect of the rental value of the flats. This list of issues is not meant to be exhaustive and the matter should be fully researched before embarking on the project so that you know whether or not the project will qualify for this relief.

The benefit of short-life assets

Items of plant and equipment that have a short life (typically four years or less) should be placed in a short-life assets pool. This will allow a balancing allowance or charge to arise if the asset is disposed of within four years. An election for this to apply to items purchased has to be made within one year after 31 January following the tax year in which the period of accounts ends in which the purchase was made. This relief will only be of benefit if your expenditure on plant and equipment exceeds £50,000 in the year.

Failure to make an election (which is irrevocable) will mean that the balancing adjustment for the disposal will only be made when the business ceases.

Use your business's losses

If you have made a loss in your business, look carefully at how best it can be utilised. Losses can be set against your general income for the year in which they arise and/or the previous year. Also, the losses can be carried forward to set against future profits of the same trade.

A template to help you prepare your figures for the self-employed part of the Tax Return

Your name _____ Accounting year end _____

Self-Employment and Partnerships

Sales income [ ] **A**

less

Costs of sales, e.g. raw materials and stocks [ ]

Construction industry subcontractors' costs [ ]

Other direct costs, e.g. packing and despatch [ ]

Total cost of sales [ ] **B**

Gross profit or loss A – B [ ] **C**

Other income [ ] **D**

Expenditure

Employee costs
Salaries, wages, bonuses, employer's NIC, pension contributions, casual wages, canteen costs, recruitment agency fees, subcontractors' (unless shown above) and other wages costs [ ]

Premises costs
Rent, ground rent, rates, water, refuse, light and heat, property insurance, security and use of home [ ]

Repairs
Repair of property, replacements, renewals, maintenance [ ]

General administrative expenses
Telephone, fax, mobile telephone, stationery, photocopying, printing, postage, courier and computer costs, subscriptions, insurance [ ]

Motoring expenses
Petrol, servicing, licence, repairs, motor insurance, hire and leasing, car parking, RAC/AA membership [ ]

Travel and subsistence
Rail, air, bus, etc., travel, taxis, subsistence and hotel costs [ ]

Entertainment
Staff entertaining (e.g. Christmas party), customer gifts up to £50 per person advertising your business [ ]

Advertising and promotion
Advertising, promotion, mailshots, free samples, brochures, newsletters, trade shows, etc. [ ]

Legal and professional costs
Accountancy, legal, architects, surveyors, stocktakers' fees, indemnity insurance [ ]

Bad debts (if already included in A above) [ ]

Interest
on bank loans, overdraft and other loans [ ]

Other finance charges
Bank charges, HP interest, credit card charges, leasing not already included [ ]

Depreciation and losses on sale (please ask for advice) [ ]

Other items – please describe [ ]

Grand total of expenses [ ] **E**

Net profit (or loss) C + D – E [ ]

In a new business the losses may also be carried back and set against general income of the previous three years, the earliest first.

A loss on cessation can be relieved against trading income of the final year and/or against trading income of the three previous years, latest first.

Ensure that you get relief not only against tax for the losses, but also against your Class 4 National Insurance contributions liability.

A loss claim can be extended to include relief against capital gains in the year of the loss and/or the previous year.

However, from 6 April 2008, for individuals carrying on a trade in a non-active capacity, i.e. spending on average less than ten hours per week on commercial activities of the trade, there is an annual limit of £25,000 for losses which can be set against other income in the year – 'sideways' loss relief.

Loss-relief claims can be quite complex, particularly if there are multiple claims. It's vital that the implications of the claims are carefully reviewed and, if necessary, professional advice taken.

49 Have you claimed for all your business expenses?

See the template on the previous page. The general rule is that all such expenses must be incurred wholly and exclusively for the purposes of the business.

50 Farmers and averaging

Farmers and market gardeners, whether trading on their own or in partnership, may average their profits over two tax years if the profit of one year is less than 70 per cent of the profit of the other year. If the profit is between 70 per cent and 75 per cent relative to the other, then there is a marginal relief available.

The purpose of this treatment is to smooth out the peaks and troughs of good and bad years. You could, for instance, be paying higher-rate tax in one year and nothing in the following year. An averaging claim, while a little complex, can be very worthwhile, as it optimises the use of personal allowances, capital allowances and agricultural building allowances. This not only minimises your tax liabilities, but also it can maximise your entitlements to tax credits and the like.

An averaging claim must be made within a year of 31 January following the end of the second tax year, and a claim cannot be made in the first or last year of trading. The averaging can continue year after year.

Partnerships

Have a proper partnership deed to prove the partnership exists and make sure there is a partnership bank account and proper letterhead for the same reason.

Partnerships can be tricky things – they are not to be entered into lightly. For one, if your partner goes bust, you could easily find that you are (what is called) 'jointly and severally liable' for each others' debts. So be very careful whom you go into partnership with.

Partnerships cannot just be set up at a whim. They need to be planned and created properly, and then they may be able to save a significant sum in tax.

What are the golden rules of partnerships and what are the things you should look out for?

The taxman may need proof that what you have created is indeed a partnership. To do this, you should be able to show him:

- a partnership bank account (with the names of the partners or at least the name of the partnership on the statements);
- letterheads, invoices, business cards, etc.;
- advertisements (as in Yellow Pages) in the name of the partnership;
- brochures, if you have them; and
- a proper partnership deed. You really should have one of these, not just to show the taxman, but as a formal record of the terms

under which you and your partner(s) agreed to go into business. If something were to go wrong (and partnerships have a habit of going wrong – partners fall out or, worse still, partners can die), it's vital to have it all recorded what the partners should do in such an eventuality.

Claiming tax relief on interest

If you borrow money to buy shares in a private company or a share in a partnership, or to buy plant and machinery for business use, you should be able to get tax relief on the interest at your top rate of tax. So if you are a higher-rate taxpayer, this will be 40 per cent. Similarly, if you borrow money to lend to a partnership of which you are a partner or company in which you are a shareholder, tax relief will be due providing you are not a limited partner or a partner in an investment limited liability partnership (i.e. a business that makes investments). If the loan is to a company, you must own at least five per cent of the issued share capital and also work there, more or less full time, in a managerial capacity.

CHAPTER 9

National Insurance

53. It may be advisable for a married woman to pay NI contributions, even though she doesn't have to

54. Get a state pension forecast well before retirement age

55. Don't pay too much National Insurance

It may be advisable for a married woman to pay NI contributions, even though she doesn't have to

If you are a married woman who elected to pay reduced-rate contributions, it may be advisable to withdraw this election to increase the amount of your state pension.

 ## Get a state pension forecast well before retirement age

If you don't qualify for the full amount, you may be able to boost your entitlement. The forecast can be obtained by filling out Form BR19, available online at www.thepensionservice.gov.uk or by phoning 0845 3000 168.

 ## Don't pay too much National Insurance

If you are employed as well as self-employed, you may be paying too much National Insurance. Consider deferring Class 2 and/or Class 4 contributions and HM Revenue & Customs (HMRC) will then check the position after the end of the tax year.

You may also be due a rebate if you have a number of employments running concurrently in the year.

CHAPTER 10
Capital Gains Tax

56. Make use of the Capital Gains Tax changes

57. Make use of the annual Capital Gains Tax exemption (1)

58. Make use of the annual Capital Gains Tax exemption (2)

59. Don't overlook claiming relief for shares that are now worthless

60. Entrepreneurs' relief

61. Assets you can sell without incurring Capital Gains Tax

62. Suggestions for investments with tax advantages

63. It can be a good idea to crystallise capital gains if there is going to be no tax to pay

64. Claim rollover relief

65. Time your sales to defer payment of Capital Gains Tax

66. Reduce or eliminate Capital Gains Tax on a second home

Make use of the Capital Gains Tax changes

The new Chancellor, Alistair Darling, has abolished indexation and taper relief and replaced these with a flat rate of 18 per cent for gains in excess of the annual exemption. This has greatly simplified the Capital Gains Tax legislation which became more and more complicated during Gordon Brown's time as Chancellor.

All you have to do now, to work out your gain, is to take the sale proceeds less any costs of sale, deduct the original cost or market value in 1982, deduct the cost of any improvements and you have the chargeable gain. Amongst those benefiting from the 18 per cent rate will be buy-to-let investors and short-term stock market investors.

 Make use of the annual Capital Gains Tax exemption (1)

In 2008/09 the Capital Gains Tax annual exemption is £9,600. If you can structure your financial affairs to give you gains each year that don't exceed this figure, you effectively have extra tax-free income. Investments giving rise to gains are most frequently unit trusts and shares, although those held in ISAs and investments in government gilts don't have any capital gains liability.

While most people accept that investments of this type can go down as well as up, if you make investments through an authorised adviser and you suffer a loss because of poor advice, poor investment management or the adviser going out of business, there is a Financial Services Compensation Scheme, which can pay compensation of up to £48,000 – for more information, visit its website at www.fscs.org.uk.

 Make use of the annual Capital Gains Tax exemption (2)

Assets transferred between spouses are exempt and each spouse is entitled to the exempt amount of £9,600 (2008/09 figure).

If there will be tax to pay, consider transferring the asset to the non-taxpaying spouse.

Transfers between spouses followed by a sale could be attacked by HM Revenue & Customs (HMRC) as an anti-avoidance measure, so there should be a delay between the transfer and the subsequent sale. There should be no strings attached to the gift whatsoever, particularly something which might result in the eventual proceeds going back to the transferor.

 ## Don't overlook claiming relief for shares that are now worthless

If you have tax to pay, check to see if you or your spouse have shares in companies that are now worthless. If you do, whatever those shares cost will equal a loss which can be offset against gains. Remember to transfer the shares to the spouse who has the gain first.

 ## Entrepreneurs' relief

If you sell your business, you may be entitled to entrepreneurs' relief. This gives preferential treatment to the disposal of business assets. This includes trading businesses either carried alone or in partnership, assets of that business, shares in the individual's own trading company and assets owned by the individual but used in their trading company or business. The relief reduces the amount of the gain chargeable to tax by 4/9ths, so that when the resulting gain is charged to tax at 18 per cent it's equivalent to ten per cent on the whole of the gain.

There is a lifetime limit of £1m upon which the entrepreneurs' relief can be claimed and claims can be made on more than one occasion to utilise the lifetime limit. The business must have been owned for at least one year ending on the date of the disposal.

Furnished holiday letting properties are also regarded as business assets, but not properties used for any other type of letting. To qualify as furnished holiday letting, the property must:

- be available as holiday accommodation for at least 140 days in a tax year; and

- be let on a commercial basis for at least 70 days; and

- not be occupied for more than 31 days by the same person in any period of seven months.

Despite a degree of simplification, this can still be a complex area and professional advice should be taken.

 ## 61 Assets you can sell without incurring Capital Gains Tax

You can sell chattels such as jewellery, pictures and furniture where the proceeds are £6,000 or less without incurring Capital Gains Tax. Please note that if you sell, say, a set of chairs for more than £6,000, you cannot claim this as being free from Capital Gains Tax on the basis that each individual chair was sold for less than £6,000. HMRC looks at the set as being the item, not the individual items themselves. Other assets you can sell (or gains you can make) without incurring Capital Gains Tax are:

- Private motor vehicles

- Your own home (but not including a second home)

- National Savings Certificates

- Foreign currency

- Decorations for gallantry (unless purchased)

- Betting winnings (including pools, lotteries and Premium Bonds)

- Compensation or damages for any wrong or injury suffered

- British Government Securities

- Life assurance policies and deferred annuities

- Chattels (i.e. movable possessions) sold for £6,000 or less

- Assets given to a charity or the nation

- Enterprise Investment Scheme shares held for three years

- Timber and uncut trees

- Individual Savings Accounts

- Venture Capital Trust shares held for five years

- Guns, wine, antiques – providing they are not used in a business

- Debts

- Qualifying Corporate Bonds

- Child Trust Funds

 # Suggestions for investments with tax advantages

While it's not our business to suggest individual investments, the following investments have certain tax advantages:

- **National Savings Certificates**

- **Children's Bonus Bonds:** these are high-interest savings schemes for children under the age of 16. You can get a brochure at any post office and both the interest and the bonus are tax free.

- **Child Trust Funds:** the government give £250 to start off and up to £1,200 can be added each year until the age of 18. The government contributes a further £250 at the age of seven. The government contributions are higher for lower income earners.

- **Enterprise Investment Scheme:** if you invest in this, Income Tax relief is given at 20 per cent up to £500,000 invested in any year. The gains are free of Capital Gains Tax. The shares must be held for at least three years. There are other rules concerning the Enterprise Investment Scheme but these are the most important ones.

- **Venture Capital Trusts:** investors are exempt from tax on dividends so long as the shares purchased did not cost more than the permitted maximum for the year of purchase. If you subscribe for up to £200,000 worth of shares, you get 30 per cent tax relief but you have to hold onto the shares for five years. Any gains are free of Capital Gains Tax.

It can be a good idea to crystallise capital gains if there is going to be no tax to pay

Each year you are entitled to make tax-free capital gains of £9,600 (2008/09 figure). If you have not made any gains and have (say) some shares that, if you were to sell them, would achieve a taxable gain of no more than £9,600, it would make sense to sell them and then buy them back (if you wanted to keep the shares) because you would then have them at a higher cost of acquisition and if you were to sell them again in the future, this would reduce or possibly eliminate any taxable gain when that happens. If you do buy the shares back, you have to wait for 30 days to do so.

 ## Claim rollover relief

If you make a gain on the sale of a qualifying business asset, and reinvest the proceeds in a new qualifying business asset, within the period starting one year before and ending three years after the original disposal, a claim may be made to have the gain deferred.

Qualifying business assets include land and buildings (including property which qualifies as furnished holiday lettings); plant and machinery; ships; aircraft; hovercraft; goodwill; milk, potato and fish quotas; ewe and suckler cow premium quotas; payment entitlements under the farmers' single payment scheme and Lloyds syndicate rights.

For the very adventurous business person, satellites, spacestations and spacecrafts are also included!

The replacement asset doesn't have to be within the same category as the asset sold.

Where only some of the sale proceeds are reinvested, the remaining part of the gain is immediately chargeable.

Time your sales to defer payment of Capital Gains Tax

A tax deferred gives you a cash-flow advantage, so it makes sense to delay the due date for paying tax whenever you can. If you sell an asset on 5 April, you will have to pay the Capital Gains Tax ten months later. If you delay the sale by just one day and sell on 6 April, the Capital Gains Tax doesn't have to be paid for 22 months. Don't forget the date of sale for Capital Gains Tax purposes is the date you exchange contracts and not the completion date.

 ## Reduce or eliminate Capital Gains Tax on a second home

If you are about to purchase or have purchased a second home, you can elect (within two years from buying the second one) which is to be the principal private residence for Capital Gains Tax purposes. This is a complex area and it's recommended that you take professional advice.

A further consideration worth looking into would be if you are selling a second home and there is tax to pay, could you occupy it for a short time as your main residence as this may reduce the tax payable? You would get a minimum of three years' worth of Private Residence Relief (but you would genuinely need to move in for a period).

There are also valuable allowances available where your main residence has been let: £40,000 for let property relief and a 36-month extension for Private Residence Relief.

CHAPTER 11
Inheritance Tax

67. Check up to see what your Inheritance Tax is likely to be

68. What gifts are exempt from Inheritance Tax?

69. Inheritance Tax business/agricultural property relief

70. Don't leave everything to your wife – use the tax-free band carefully

(67) Check up to see what your Inheritance Tax is likely to be

I own	Estimated value	At my death I would like to leave this to:
House		
Valuables		
Shares*		
Cash		
Other land and property		
Trust		
Business assets*		
The residue of my estate		
Legacies I would like to give		Details:
Substantial gifts I have made in the last seven years		Gifted to:
Less Sums I owe	( )	How will these be repaid on death?
Total estate		
Less tax-free band	(312,000)	
Less unused tax-free band of deceased spouse/civil partner (only available when the second death is after 8 October 2007)	(x)	
Total net		
Tax due @ 40%		

*Some shares (those listed on the Alternative Investment Market and shares in unlisted companies) and business assets will attract 100 per cent business property relief and be effectively free of Inheritance Tax.

What gifts are exempt from Inheritance Tax?

Many gifts are exempt from tax so make use of these exemptions.

- Gifts between spouses, but if one spouse is not UK domiciled, the lifetime exemption is limited to £55,000.

- Gifts of up to £3,000 in each tax year are exempt and the unused portion of the previous year's exemption can be carried forward but only for one year.

- A gift of £250 to any one person if the total gifts to that person don't exceed £250. This can be used to cover Christmas and birthday gifts from grandparents to grandchildren.

- Wedding gifts of up to:

  - £5,000 from each parent to each child;

  - £2,500 from each grandparent;

  - £1,000 from anybody else.

  The gift must be made shortly before the marriage and becomes effective when the marriage takes place.

- If you have surplus income year on year, this can be gifted free of Inheritance Tax. You need to be able to show that such gifts are part of your regular annual expenditure and don't reduce your standard of living. The exemption can be used if you pay life insurance premiums for the benefit of someone else. You should keep a record of these gifts and if possible a record of your net (after tax) income. This can be a very useful exemption as there is no upper limit so it's worth keeping the documentation.

- Gifts to UK charities, political parties (providing they have at least one MP and 150,000 votes), registered housing associations and gifts for national purposes are also exempt.

- Maintenance payments to your dependants and ex-spouse.

If the gift is not covered by any of these exemptions, then providing you survive for seven years it will be free of Inheritance Tax.

Inheritance Tax business/agricultural property relief

Certain categories of business and business assets may qualify for 100 per cent exemption from Inheritance Tax after two years. The relief normally applies to a business or an interest in a business (partnership) or to shares in an unlisted company. Shares quoted on the Alternative Investment Market also qualify after two years. The exemption also applies to farmers after two years if they farm the land and after seven years if the farm is let to someone else who farms the land. Full details of these reliefs are beyond the scope of this book and professional advice should be taken.

 ## Changes to the tax-free band

The new Chancellor, Alistair Darling in his first Pre-Budget Report announced that from 9 October 2007, married couples or civil registered partners will inherit each other's unused element of the nil-rate band on first death. So, each couple will have a joint nil-rate band of £624,000. This will increase to £700,000 in 2010–2011. If the couple's joint estate falls within the joint nil-rate band, they no longer have to worry about Inheritance Tax. Although this was possible to achieve before 9 October 2007, it involved setting up complicated Wills and trusts.

For everyone else including unmarried couples, siblings living together and carers who have lived with and inherited the family home, the nil-rate band is £312,000, rising to £350,000 in 2010–2011.

CHAPTER 12
Overseas aspects

71. Can you save tax by going abroad?

71 Can you save tax by going abroad?

Residence, domicile, etc.

The overseas aspects of UK taxation is a complex area, but, in general terms, if you are a UK resident, you will be liable to UK tax on your world income. If you are not a UK resident, you will only be liable to pay UK tax on income arising in the UK.

Without wanting to make matters too complex, reference will be made to the terms residence, ordinary residence and domicile.

Residence

You will always be a UK resident if you spend 183 days per year in the UK excluding the days of arrival and departure. Being in the UK for less than 183 days per year does **not** automatically mean that you are not resident. It's possible to be resident in more than one country at a time.

Ordinary residence

If you are generally resident in the UK year after year, even though on occasion you may not be resident for a particular tax year, then you are ordinarily resident.

Domicile

A person's domicile is usually the country in which they have their permanent home and other related connections. When you are born you usually take your father's domicile ('domicile of origin'). Until you are able to change it, you will follow the domicile of the person on whom you are dependent ('domicile of dependency'). It's also possible to change your domicile by moving to another country and thoroughly embedding yourself within the society and culture ('domicile of choice'). There are high standards of proof for this, however.

The domicile of married women is now determined independently of their husbands.

Leaving the UK

Strictly speaking, you are resident or not resident for a complete tax year. By concession you can split your year of departure into resident up to the date of departure and non-resident from that date. When leaving the UK you should complete Form P85 and if it's your intention to be abroad for at least one complete tax year, you will be treated as provisionally non-resident. You must not be in the UK for more than 183 days in any year and the average number of days in the UK over the period of your absence must not exceed 91 days per year. Periods spent in the UK for exceptional reasons (e.g. serious illness) are usually ignored.

Providing you establish and maintain your non-resident status, any earnings abroad of a UK person won't be liable to UK Income Tax.

There are, however, special rules for Crown employees (e.g. civil servants, diplomats, members of the armed forces, etc.) and these people should refer to HM Revenue & Customs (HMRC) for clarification of their position.

There are special rules relating to seafarers and aircrew. Seafarers may be eligible for a Foreign Earnings Deduction, but this matter should be explored with HMRC.

Arriving in the UK

If you arrive in the UK, you are treated as resident and ordinarily resident from your date of arrival if you intend to live here permanently or actually remain here for more than three complete tax years. Form P86 should be completed and submitted to HMRC. Issues of what you intend and subsequently what you actually do in terms of the time spent in the UK are both very important. Matters will be reviewed each year and after four years it will be possible to decide definitely what an individual's residence status is. Being treated as resident and ordinarily resident will bring an entitlement to UK personal allowances – see the Appendix.

Non-residents cannot claim UK personal allowances unless they are UK, Commonwealth or Republic of Ireland citizens or EEA nationals (EU countries plus Iceland, Norway and Liechtenstein).

If you are UK resident and domiciled and in receipt of a pension from overseas, you can claim a ten per cent deduction on the amount of pension liable to tax in the UK.

People becoming non-resident in the UK but retaining a property here which is going to be let out become non-resident landlords. HMRC needs to be notified on Form NRL1. HMRC can authorise the rents to be paid without the deduction of basic-rate tax, by the letting agent or the tenant, which is what should happen automatically. Provided the landlord is within one of the categories above, a claim for UK personal allowances can be made to minimise tax liabilities.

Non-residents who are in receipt of the UK state pension can disclaim personal allowances and have the full amount of state pension removed from their tax liability calculations.

If an individual left the UK after 17 March 1998 and has been non-resident for five complete tax years from the date of departure, there is no liability to Capital Gains Tax on assets sold prior to their return to the UK.

If you are resident but not domiciled in the UK, or resident but not ordinarily resident in the UK and a Commonwealth citizen (includes UK) or a citizen of the Republic of Ireland, you will be taxed on income remitted to the UK (i.e. paid to the UK). Because this was seen as a way of avoiding tax, those wishing to pay tax on the remittance basis, who have been resident in the UK for more than seven of the past ten years, will have to pay an annual charge of £30,000 with effect from 6 April 2008. Domicile is a highly complex area and anyone affected by the change should seek professional help.

Queries on overseas and residence issues are best directed to HMRC at the Centre for Non-Residents, Residence Advice and Liabilities (Unit 355), St Johns House, Merton Road, Bootle, Merseyside L69 9BB; tel. 0845 070 0040.

Scope of liability to Income Tax of earnings

		Duties of Employment Performed Wholly or Partly in the UK		Duties of Employment Performed Wholly Outside the UK
		In the UK	*Outside the UK*	
Foreign Emoluments[1]	Employee resident and ordinarily resident in the UK	Liable – less possible deduction[2]	Liable – less possible deduction[2]	Liable if received in the UK[3]
	Resident but not ordinarily resident	Liable	Liable if received in the UK[3]	Liable if received in the UK[3]
	Not resident	Liable	Not liable	Not liable
Other Earnings	Resident and ordinarily resident	Liable – less possible deduction[2]	Liable – less possible deduction[2]	Liable – less possible deduction[2]
	Resident but not ordinarily resident	Liable	Liable if received in the UK[3]	Liable if received in the UK[3]
	Not resident	Liable	Not liable	Not liable

1. 'Foreign emoluments' is the term used in the Taxes Act to mean the earnings of someone who is not domiciled in the UK and whose employer is resident outside, and not resident in, the UK (nor resident in the Republic of Ireland).

2. There may be a foreign earnings deduction of 100 per cent in these cases from the amount chargeable, if the earnings are for a period which is part of a qualifying absence lasting 365 days or more – this means that such earnings for that period will be free from UK tax. This only applies to seafarers.

3. The remittance basis which applies in these cases. See page 76.

Scope of liability to Income Tax on individuals receiving pensions

	Paid by or on Behalf of a Person	
	In the UK	Outside the UK (Overseas Pension)
Residence Status and Domicile		
Resident and ordinarily resident, and domiciled	Liable	Liable[1]
Resident and ordinarily resident, not domiciled	Liable	Liable if received in the UK[2,6]
Resident but not ordinarily resident, domiciled	Liable	Liable[1,3]
Resident but not ordinarily resident, not domiciled	Liable	Liable if received in the UK[2,6]
Not resident	Liable[4,5]	Not liable

1. Less ten per cent deduction.

2. You are taxable on the whole of a pension arising in the Republic of Ireland, less ten per cent deduction; but if the pension is from the Irish Government, you are taxable only if you are a UK national without also being an Irish national.

3. If you are a Commonwealth (this includes British) citizen or an Irish citizen, the remittance basis applies and the ten per cent deduction is not due, unless the pension arises in the Irish Republic, in which case note 2 applies.

4. There may be relief under a double taxation agreement.

5. It may be beneficial not to claim UK personal allowances.

6. If you are not UK domiciled and opt for the remittance basis of taxation, there may be an annual charge of £30,000. See page 76.

Scope of liability to Income Tax on profits of individuals carrying on a trade or profession

Residence Status and Domicile	Trade or Profession Carried on Wholly or Partly in the UK	Trade or Profession Carried on Wholly Outside the UK
Resident and ordinarily resident, and domiciled	Liable	Liable
Resident and ordinarily resident, not domiciled	Liable	Liable if received in the UK[1,4]
Resident but not ordinarily resident, domiciled	Liable	Liable[2]
Resident but not ordinarily resident, not domiciled	Liable	Liable if received in the UK[1,4]
Not resident	Liable[3]	Not liable

1. You are taxable on the whole of the income from a trade or profession carried on wholly in the Republic of Ireland.

2. If you are a Commonwealth (this includes British) citizen or an Irish citizen, the remittance basis applies unless the trade or profession is carried on wholly in the Irish Republic, in which case note 1 applies.

3. You are liable on the profits of the part of the trade or profession carried on in the UK.

4. If you are not UK domiciled and opt for the remittance basis of taxation, there may be an annual charge of £30,000. See page 76.

CHAPTER 13

When someone dies

72. Don't overpay Inheritance Tax on assets that are sold

73. Remember to claim full probate costs when someone dies

74. Capital Gains Tax and Inheritance Tax considerations

72 Don't overpay Inheritance Tax on assets that are sold

Inheritance Tax is a damaging tax. Not only is the rate high (40 per cent) and the sums payable tend to have a great many noughts after them, but, on top of this, the tax has to be paid from a bank account that probably has no cash in it with which to pay the tax. It's what can be called an 'ouch'.

There are few ameliorations of this dreadful state of affairs but there is one and it's often overlooked.

Inheritance Tax is paid on the probate value of the assets. This is the professional value that is put on the assets as at the date of death. But if you sell certain of these assets within either four years of death for land and property (one year for quoted securities) and they realise a sum that is lower than probate, you can apply to the Capital Taxes Office for a refund of 40 per cent of the difference between the two. You can only get the relief if there is an overall loss on the sale of quoted securities. The relief is not due solely on the shares that have realised a loss.

While on this subject, if the asset is sold for a higher sum, then remember that Capital Gains Tax may be payable.

73 Remember to claim full probate costs when someone dies

When an asset is to be sold by the personal representatives of the deceased, the cost will be its probate value. This can be increased further to make some allowance for probate costs. The amount allowed is based on the size of the estate and ranges from 1.8 per cent if the estate is valued at up to £50,000 to 0.16 per cent for estates valued over £5,000,000, subject to a maximum of £10,000.

74 Capital Gains Tax and Inheritance Tax considerations

If elderly people are considering giving away their assets to reduce

Inheritance Tax, bear in mind that there is no Capital Gains Tax to pay on death and the beneficiaries will inherit assets at probate value. This could be considerably higher than the value at the time of the gift so the beneficiaries may be able to sell the asset after death without incurring Capital Gains Tax. This needs careful planning as you could end up paying more Inheritance Tax than the Capital Gains Tax saved.

If an asset that belonged to someone who has died is sold, there could be Capital Gains Tax due on the gain, but estates of deceased persons can claim the annual exemption (£9,600 for 2008/09) for not only the tax year in which they died but the following two years as well. Thereafter, no exemption is available.

CHAPTER 14
Pensions

75. Take out a pension

76. You may be able to take out a pension even if you are not earning

Take out a pension

If you contribute to a pension scheme, the government will add a further £2.50 for every £10 you pay and if you are a higher-rate taxpayer, the government contribution increases to £6.66. And don't forget, once the money is invested it grows in a tax-free environment with one exception. Unfortunately, the government will no longer repay the ten per cent tax credit attached to dividends paid to your accumulating fund.

 ## You may be able to take out a pension even if you are not earning

Stakeholder pensions are not just for workers. Non-earning spouses and children can have a stakeholder pension and benefit from 20 per cent tax relief. So for higher-rate taxpayers, this is a useful way of sheltering your capital from Income Tax and investing it in a tax-free environment for the benefit of your family.

The maximum contribution is £3,600 per annum before tax relief which equates to a net payment of £2,880.

CHAPTER 15

Property

77. Rent a room

78. VAT and rent

79. Have you claimed for all the expenses you can?

80. Claim the interest on any loan you take out to buy the property

81. Do you and your wife jointly own the property?

82. Forestry

77 Rent a room

You can receive gross rents of up to £4,250 tax free per year for letting furnished rooms in your own home. If you own two properties, the relief only applies to the main family home. If the property is jointly owned, the relief is divided between you. Should the rent you receive exceed this amount, you have two choices. You can choose to pay tax on the excess rent over £4,250 or on the rent you receive less the expenses. You have to make a claim if you want to pay on the excess over £4,250 and this basis will apply until you withdraw the claim. This relief is usually used when people take in lodgers so it won't apply if the rooms you let comprise of a flat with its own facilities. If the rent is within the rent-a-room scheme, there won't be any Capital Gains Tax issues if you ever sell your house. The relief is also available to people running a bed & breakfast business.

The relief is not just for owner-occupiers. If you are a tenant in rented accommodation, you will also qualify if you sublet a room, providing that it's your main home.

It's advisable to tell your mortgage company and your insurers if you enter into a rent-a-room arrangement.

78 VAT and rent

If you are VAT registered and you also have rental income, you are making what the VAT man calls an 'exempt' supply. You cannot charge VAT on the rent and equally you cannot reclaim VAT on the property expenses. Normally, a partly exempt business has to use a special method to work out how much VAT it can reclaim. However, if the input tax on the property expenses in any VAT period is not more than:

1. £625 per month on average; and

2. one half of all input tax for the period concerned;

all the input tax on the property expenses can be reclaimed.

The above doesn't apply if you receive rents from non-domestic property and you have chosen to tax these rents.

79 Have you claimed for all the expenses you can?

See the template on the following page.

 80 Claim the interest on any loan you take out to buy the property

If you borrow money to buy a property to let, you will get tax relief on the interest you pay at your top rate of tax. You can also get tax relief on loans to fund improvements, alterations or repairs.

There is an interesting addition to the manuals of HM Revenue & Customs (HMRC) which indicates that interest on funds borrowed for private purposes may be deductible against rental income in certain circumstances. This has wide-reaching implications for buy-to-let investors.

One example in the manual covers Mr A, who owns a flat in London and is moving abroad. He decides to let the property while he is away. During his period of ownership, the property has trebled in value. He renegotiates the mortgage to convert it to a buy-to-let mortgage and borrows a further amount which he uses to buy a property overseas. Can he claim tax relief on the interest against the rents? Well, HMRC says that owners of businesses (and renting property is a business for tax purposes) are entitled to withdraw their capital from the business, even though substitute funding then has to be provided by interest-bearing loans. In the case of Mr A, his opening balance sheet shows the following:

Original mortgage	80,000	**Property at market value**	375,000
Capital account	295,000		
	£375,000		£375,000

When Mr A renegotiates his mortgage, he borrows a further £125,000, which goes through his property business. He then withdraws this amount to fund the purchase of the property overseas. By the end of the first year of letting, his balance sheet shows the following.

A template to help you prepare your figures for the Land and Property pages of the Tax Return

Your name _____

Land and Property Income (year to 5 April   )

Income   Received from   Rents received
                                                                £

_____

_____

_____

                                        Total income   £

                    Tax already deducted from property income   £

                                              £   £

Expenditure   **Premises** Rents _____
                                    Rates _____
                          Property insurance _____
                            Light and heat _____
                                  Cleaning _____
                                  Security _____
                                              Subtotal [   ]

       Repairs and maintenance Repairs and renewals _____
                              Redecorating _____
                               Small tools _____
                                              Subtotal [   ]

  Finance charges and interest on loan to buy rented property [   ]

              Legal and professional Legal _____
                                Accountancy _____
                             Debt collection _____
                            Other insurances _____
                              Subscriptions _____
                            Architects' fees _____
                                              Subtotal [   ]

              Services provided Wages _____
                                 Telephone _____
                                        TV _____
                                    Garden _____
                                     Roads _____
                                              Subtotal [   ]

              Other costs Advertising _____
                                Agents' fees _____
                                Office costs _____
                                     Travel _____
                                              Subtotal [   ]

                                  Total expenditure [£   ]

Mortgage	205,000	Property at market value	375,000
Capital account b/f	295,000		
Less drawings	(125,000)		
Carry forward	170,000		
	£375,000		£375,000

Although he has withdrawn capital from the business, the interest on the mortgage loan is allowable in full because it's funding the transfer of the property to the business at its open market value at the time the business started. Although HMRC's example has a further mortgage of £125,000, it seems that Mr A could withdraw a further £170,000 of tax-allowable finance. However, he should not take out more than he puts in as his capital account will be in the red (i.e. overdrawn).

The best advice is not to assume that you will automatically get tax relief but to take professional advice before you remortgage.

 ## 81 Do you and your wife jointly own the property?

If a husband and wife own a property in joint names (joint tenancy), the income and expenditure is always divided equally when filling in the Tax Return forms. However, if the ownership is owned as tenants in common and if you ask the tax office for Form 17, you can jointly declare the ownership split that actually applies and then you can enter those amounts on the Tax Returns.

 ## 82 Forestry

Forestry can be a good way to save tax. In principle, there are three main advantages:

1. There is no Inheritance Tax on forestry.

2. There is no Income Tax on forestry.

3. When it comes to forestry sales, only the land, not growing timber, attracts Capital Gains Tax.

There may not be much money in forestry, but at least there's virtually no tax either!

CHAPTER 16
Savings

83. Remember to claim back tax deducted from deposit interest

84. ISAs and investments

85. Premium savings bonds

Remember to claim back tax deducted from deposit interest

If you are not a taxpayer, i.e. your annual taxable income is less than your personal allowances (see number 10), you can elect to have any bank or building society interest you receive to be paid without tax being deducted. In the majority of cases, and in the absence of such an election, interest is paid after 20 per cent tax has been deducted and it's 'net' interest rather than 'gross'. If you are not a taxpayer (or only liable at ten per cent) but have suffered tax on your interest, then you will be due a refund.

84 ISAs and investments

Most people will have heard of Individual Savings Accounts (ISAs), which allow interest to be paid tax free. Shares can also be held in an ISA and these can be sold free of Capital Gains Tax. There are, however, various maximum limits applicable, which are as follows from 6 April 2008:

- The annual ISA investment allowance will be raised to £7,200. Up to £3,600 of that allowance can be saved in cash with one provider. The remainder of the £7,200 can be invested in stocks and shares with either the same or a different provider.

- ISA savers will be able to invest in two separate ISAs each tax year; a cash ISA and a stocks and shares ISA. Mini and maxi ISAs will no longer exist.

- Mini cash ISAs, TESSA-only ISAs (TOISAs) and the cash component of a maxi ISA will automatically become cash ISAs.

- Mini stocks and shares ISAs and the stocks and shares component of a maxi ISA will automatically become stocks and shares ISAs.

- All Personal Equity Plans (PEPs) will automatically become stocks and shares ISAs.

- ISA savers will be able to transfer money saved in their cash ISA to their stocks and shares ISA.

There is also a range of National Savings investments available, but these can involve locking your capital away for a fixed period and there is also a maximum amount that can be invested each year. National Savings Certificates should be considered as the interest is paid tax free. Therefore, the interest rates paid can be attractive to higher-rate taxpayers. Pensioners who would have their age-related allowances reduced by receiving taxable income should also give consideration to tax-free investments (those with taxable incomes over £21,800 in 2008/09).

85 Premium savings bonds

If you like a flutter but don't want to risk your capital, premium bonds may be for you. The minimum investment is £100 and the maximum holding is £30,000. The monthly draw results in prizes of various amounts which are tax free. As well as two £1 million jackpots, you can win anything from £50 to £100,000 for each bond number you hold. You can encash the bonds at any time for face value.

CHAPTER 17
Charitable giving

86. Gift Aid

87. Charities

86 Gift Aid

If you 'Gift Aid' a donation to charity, the charity claims back the basic-rate tax that is deemed to have been deducted from the grossed-up payment. Therefore, for every pound you Gift Aid to charity, the charity claims an additional 28p. (However, you must have paid at least 25p in tax yourself.) Although the basic rate band is 20 per cent from 6 April 2008, charities will be able to reclaim 28p for every pound gifted up to 5 April 2011.

In addition to feeling good about your generosity, if you are a higher-rate taxpayer, you are also entitled to tax relief at an additional 20 per cent on your donation. This is achieved by extending your basic-rate band, i.e. more of your income is charged to tax at 20 per cent rather than 40 per cent. You can also elect for your gift to be treated as paid in the previous tax year so that higher-rate relief can be claimed in that year.

87 Charities

As well as cash gifts to charities, tax relief is also available on gifts of shares, securities (including AIM shares, unit trusts, etc.) and land and buildings. Individuals will get Income Tax relief on the market value of the gift on the date of the gift, plus any incidental costs of disposal or transfer, less any consideration or benefit received, at their top rate of tax. In addition, companies can claim relief. Such gifts to charities are exempt from Capital Gains Tax so neither a chargeable gain nor allowable loss will arise. Care is needed if the gift is a building on which capital allowances have been claimed as this is likely to result in a tax liability which would reduce the value of the tax relief otherwise due.

CHAPTER 18

Marriage and children

88. Give children assets when they are not worth very much

89. What are the best investments for children?

90. Plan separation and divorce carefully

Give children assets when they are not worth very much

This is one of those points which, while obvious, often gets overlooked. Let's say that you are setting up a new business and it's to be a limited company. (This is not the only sort of opportunity to which this idea might relate but it happens to make the point very well.)

So you have just incorporated the business, it hasn't yet traded and is worth extremely little. If you were to give some shares to your children on day one and if we assume that the business does well and in a few years' time it's worth a tidy sum of money, the capital growth will all belong to the children.

If, however, you delay giving them the shares, then when you transfer them to the children, you may have to pay Capital Gains Tax on the gift.

 ## What are the best investments for children?

The simplest answer is that savings accounts with building societies or banks that are in the children's names should pay the children interest gross (i.e. without tax deducted).

It's still quite permissible for children to hold shares in companies, even though the tax credits on the dividends are not refundable.

If the children don't have any investments and if the parents have surplus after-tax income of their own which they give to their children, this is usually tax free in the children's hands and if the parents are particularly wealthy, is a very useful way of transferring income to them, so that the children can accumulate a sum that can then be invested. However, once the income from the source exceeds £100 per annum, it will be taxed in the hands of the parents. If parents transfer their own shares to their children and the children are under 18, the income arising on these shares will be regarded as belonging to the parents, so this doesn't save tax.

The Child Trust Fund is available to all children born on or after 1 September 2002. The government contributes £250 when the child is born and a further £250 when the child is seven years old. Children in families receiving Child Tax Credit with a household income not exceeding £15,575 (2008/09) will receive an extra payment.

Since 1 April 2007 an extra £100 per year will be paid to every child who spends the year in care.

Parents, family and friends can contribute a further £1,200 annually. There is no Income Tax or Capital Gains Tax on the account and the child is entitled to the fund at the age of 18 and there is no restriction on how the money is used.

Plan separation and divorce carefully

Assets transferred between married couples who are living together are exempt from Capital Gains Tax. This exemption also applies in the tax year in which they separate. Arranging for the division and transfer of assets can be a time-consuming process and it's not always possible to finalise this before the end of the tax year of separation, even if separation occurs very early in the tax year. When assets are transferred after the year of separation, Capital Gains Tax is charged in the normal way. This should be borne in mind when considering a matrimonial settlement.

CHAPTER 19
And finally...

91. Free HMRC explanatory pamphlets – a good source of tax information

92. Tax planning do's

93. Tax planning don'ts

91 Free HMRC explanatory pamphlets – a good source of tax information

A number of leaflets have been discontinued and replaced either by help-sheets or guidance which can be accessed via the HM Revenue & Customs (HMRC) website (www.hmrc.gov.uk).

Information can also be obtained by visiting Enquiry Centres. HMRC is currently going through a period of reorganisation and transition. Access to HMRC staff for face-to-face discussions is becoming limited and in many cases will only be possible by prior appointment. Certain offices will be equipped with helpline phones and some may have internet access to the HMRC website.

It's strongly recommended that your starting point should be a phonecall to the phone number shown on any correspondence you have received from HMRC, or from your telephone directory. You will then be offered access to various resources which may, under certain circumstances, include a visit to a local HMRC office.

However, a word of warning. If you are expecting HMRC staff to offer a free accountancy/taxation service, you will be very disappointed.

IR8	Solicitor's Office Enforcement Section: Winding-up petitions (2002)
CIS340	Construction Industry Scheme – 6 April 2007
IR20	Residents and non-residents – Liability to tax in the UK (1999)
IR56	Employed or self-employed? A guide to employment status for tax and NI (2004)
IR109	Employer compliance reviews and negotiations (2002)
IR111	Bank and building society interest – Are you paying tax when you don't need to? (2006)
IR115	Income Tax, National Insurance Contributions and childcare (2007)
IR121	Approaching retirement – A guide to tax and NI contributions (2006)
IR160	HMRC enquiries under self-assessment (2004)
IR177	Share Incentive Plan and your entitlement to benefits (2001)
SD7	SDLT: Penalties for late land transaction returns (2004)

SD8	Enquiries under SDLT – How settlements are negotiated
480	Expenses and benefits – A tax guide (2005)
490	Employee travel – A tax and NICs guide for employers (2003)
C/FS	Complaints and putting things right
AO1	The Adjudicators' Office for complaints about HMRC and Valuation Office Agency (2006)
CH24A	Child Benefit and Guardian's Allowance – If you think our decision is wrong (2003)
CTSA/BK4	A general guide to Corporation Tax Self-Assessment (2003)
FS1	Married Couple's Allowance restrictions (2002)
FEU50	A guide to paying foreign entertainers (2000)
SE/1	Are you thinking of working for yourself? (2005)
SA/BK4	Self-assessment – A general guide to keeping records (2003)
SA/BK8	Self-assessment – Your guide (2004)
WTC1	Child Tax Credit and Working Tax Credit: An introduction (2004)
WTC2	Child Tax Credit and Working Tax Credit: A guide (2005)
WTC5	Help with the costs of childcare – Information for parents and childcare providers (2006)
WTC6	Child Tax Credit and Working Tax Credit: Other types of help you may be able to get (2006)
WTC7	Tax Credits penalties: What happens at the end of a check (2006)
WTC/FS1	Tax Credits enquiry (2006)
WTC/FS2	Tax Credits examinations (2006)
WTC/FS3	Tax Credits formal request for information (2006)
WTC/FS4	Tax Credits meetings (2006)
WTC AP	How to appeal against a Tax Credit decision or award (2004)
COP 26	What happens if we have paid you too much Tax Credit? (2006)

Business Economic Notes*

1	Travel Agents (1990)
2	Road Haulage (1995)
3	The Lodging Industry (1990)

4	Hairdressers (1990)
5	Waste Materials Reclamation and Disposal (1990)
6	Funeral Directors (1990)
7	Dentists (1990)
8	Florists (1990)
9	Licensed Victuallers (1988)
10	The Jewellery Trade (2001)
11	Electrical Retailers (1990)
12	Antiques and Fine Art Dealers (1990)
13	Fish and Chip Shops (1990)
14	The Pet Industry (1990)
15	Veterinary Surgeons (1990)
16	Catering – General (1990)
17	Catering – Restaurants (1990)
18	Catering – Fast Foods, Cafes and Snack-Bars (1990)
19	Farming – Stock Valuation for IT Purposes (1993)
20	Insurance Brokers and Agents (1994)
21	Residential Rest and Nursing Homes (1994)
22	Dispensing Chemists (1995)
23	Driving Instructors (1997)
24	Independent Fishmongers (1997)
25	Taxicabs and Private Hire Vehicles (1997)
26	Confectioners, Tobacconists and Newsagents (1997)

*These are being replaced by Tactical and Information Packages (TIPs). Those currently issued cover estate agents, mortgage brokers, franchises, confectioners, tobacconists, newsagents, and waste disposal and land fill sites.

HMRC Tax Bulletin

Published bi-monthly and freely available on the internet.

National Insurance contributions leaflets

The leaflets listed below are issued by HMRC and are available free of charge. Most are available on HMRC's internet site at www.hmrc.gov.uk or can be obtained from your local HMRC office.

CF10	NIC for self-employed people with small earnings (2005–6)
CA04	Class 2 and Class 3 NIC – Direct Debit –The easier way to pay (2004)
CF9	Widow's application for a certificate of election of reduced liability (2005)
CA17	Employee's guide to minimum contributions (2005)
CA33	Employer's Manual on Class 1A NICs on cars and fuel (2005)
CA37	Simplified Deductions Scheme for employers (2005)
CA42	Foreign-Going Mariners' Deep-Sea Fisherman's contributions for employers (2005)
CA44	NI for Company Directors (2005)
CA72A	Deferring Class 1 NIC (2007)
CA72B	Deferring self-employed NIC (2006)
CA75	Resolving Benefit Involved Cases (2001)
CA82	If you think our decision is wrong (2006)
CA89	Payroll Cleansing – A free service offered by HMRC (2003)
CA93	Shortfall in your NICs – To pay or not to pay (2005)
CA5603	To pay voluntary NI contributions (2006)
CWG2	Employer's further guide to PAYE and NICs (2005)
CWG5	Class 1A NICs on benefits in kind – A guide for employers (2005)
NI38	Social Security abroad – NICs, Social Security Benefits, Healthcare in certain overseas countries (2004)

92 Tax planning do's

- Buy your own house as soon as you can. Historically, houses have been a good investment. Any capital gain on your principal private residence will be tax free. However, by the same token there are no tax allowances for any losses on sale.

- Make sure you have got good pension and life assurance cover and keep the situation constantly under review.

- Make use (if you can afford to) of the £3,000 tax-free annual capital transfer (i.e. give this sum away Inheritance-Tax-free each year) and if you did not use up last year's allowance, you can give away an additional £3,000.

- Always claim your personal and other tax allowances. This should normally be dealt with for you by HMRC, but you should keep the matter under annual review (e.g. have you passed retirement age? This is relevant because all sorts of considerations need to be taken into account, such as increased personal allowances and the fact that you will be receiving a state pension).

- Claim all business expenses you are entitled to against any business profits – always keep a chit for petty cash expenses. If you don't, how will your accountant know you have incurred that particular expense?

- Pay your spouse properly for any work they do in your business. In the 2008/09 tax year, remember that they can earn £6,035 tax free, although payments over this sum will involve them paying National Insurance contributions.

- Consult with your stockbroker in order to make sure you take advantage of the annual £9,600 Capital Gains Tax exempt amount, i.e. if you can make a gain of this size, it will be tax free.

- Make a Will. You can create one inexpensively using Lawpack's *DIY Last Will & Testament Kit* or you can take legal advice.

- Think carefully about providing funds to pay any Inheritance Tax on death (term assurance isn't very expensive).

- Plan ahead and, wherever possible, let your accountant know in advance of your plans/wishes so that you can be advised on any tax implications.

- Divide your assets and income with your spouse so that the best use is made of the independent taxation rules.

- Let an independent financial adviser give you the equivalent of a financial 'medical examination'.

- Ask your accountant to give a rough idea of your tax liability in January and July each year. Then divide the sum by 12 and start saving up for it by transferring the monthly figure to a deposit account. This way paying tax is much less painful.

93 Tax planning don'ts

- Don't enter into tax saving schemes, on the advice of either an accountant or anyone else, that run a long time. The law can change, your circumstances can change and either could make a nonsense of a long-term plan.

- Don't automatically trust trusts – refer to Lawpack's *Tax Answers at a Glance* book if you want more information on this matter. Be very careful about putting your money into trusts – don't set them up unless they will do exactly what you want. Trusts, which are set up to protect assets from the ravages of tax, can result not only in tax having to be paid, but also in assets having to be sold to pay the tax. The net result can be ghastly. Some trusts are very useful but tread very carefully – take professional advice.

- Don't give all your money away in order to save Inheritance Tax. If you do, what will you live on?

- Don't make your affairs too complicated. Keep your affairs simple and flexible so that you can (a) understand what is going on and (b) make any changes as and when you want.

- Don't try to cheat the taxman. Be honest in all your dealings. Keep proper records of all your transactions, especially cash receipts, and declare everything properly. If you don't, you will be found out.

CHAPTER 20

A summary

94 Employees, employers and company directors

- **Shares:** companies can offer shares to staff through a share option or share incentive scheme. The rules are complicated, but the chances of acquiring wealth in a tax-efficient way are real. Talk to an accountant first.

- **Company car:** this still is the most popular fringe benefit, but the taxable benefit of having a car has increased so much in recent years that it's often better to give back the car and have the extra salary instead. However, if you are prepared to drive a smaller highly fuel-efficient car, it may still be beneficial to have a company car.

- **Company fuel:** this is now so heavily taxed that it will rarely be beneficial for a company to provide fuel to its employees. You should ensure that there is an agreement in writing which requires you to reimburse your company for any private fuel used. Better still, buy your own fuel and reclaim from the company that which is used for business.

- **Cheap loans to employees:** no taxable benefit arises in the case of an interest free or low interest loan of up to £5,000.

- **Meals:** in general, all benefits are taxable, but meals provided free of charge (or at low cost) in a canteen on the firm's premises are not taxable if they are available to staff generally.

- **Parties:** the practice of HM Revenue & Customs (HMRC) is not to tax expenditure of up to £150 per head on the annual Christmas party or a similar function, as long as it's open to all staff.

- **Accommodation:** a company may purchase a house for an employee to live in rent free. There may be tax due on the value of the accommodation, etc., but the charge will be small in proportion to the benefits provided.

- **Payments to private healthcare schemes:** these are not taxable for lower-paid employees (defined as those receiving under £8,500 per annum, including the payments).

- **Employee rewards:** tax is not payable on financial rewards to staff for suggestions they may make on the running of a business. However, such 'suggestion schemes' must meet certain requirements.

- **Incentive awards:** employees can be given non-cash awards for meeting certain targets and, in addition, any tax that these might attract can be paid by the employer on the employees' behalf.

- **Pension schemes:** these speak for themselves and their benefits are well understood. Employers can consider making pension schemes non-contributory. This way they can reduce payments they make to staff by the amount of the pension contributions the staff members have been making (in other words, the member of staff would be no worse off as a result of this), but the company would have less National Insurance contributions to pay on the lower salary figure.

- **Company directors' National Insurance contributions:** directors will be able to save themselves National Insurance contributions if, instead of receiving their pay in the form of salary, they were to receive the equivalent sum in the form of (a) rent for the company's use of property owned by them; (b) dividends on shares; or (c) interest from the loan made by them to the company. However, you should seek professional advice.

- **Loans to directors:** it's illegal under company law for a company to lend any director money and, even if it's done, there are heavy tax penalties attached to this. Do consider the following points:

  1. Immediately before incorporation the business can take out a bank loan enabling you to withdraw a substantial sum in advance.

  2. You can arrange the capital structure of the company so that at least part of your investment is by way of a loan account against which you may be free to draw.

  3. It may be possible to keep certain assets (e.g. property used by the business) outside the company.

- **Other benefits:** provide tax-free benefits to your employees such as childcare, sports or recreation facilities.

Those moving house or changing jobs

If you move home in order to take up new employment, or even a new post within your existing organisation, the following costs can be reimbursed by your employer without any Income Tax charge arising, up to an overall maximum of £8,000:

1. Bridging finance
2. Legal and professional fees, and stamp duty
3. Travel and hotel costs
4. A reasonable subsistence allowance
5. A disturbance allowance (e.g. removal costs and insurance)

Those who are about to retire or who have retired

Golden handshakes – advance tax planning:

- You might ask your employer to pay part of any payment over £30,000 into your pension (within the limits of the scheme). HMRC accepts that no tax charge arises on such payments and this could enhance the tax-free lump sum you receive from the scheme.

- If you are retiring and your total income will be significantly lower after retirement, it may be better to retire shortly after 5 April so that the taxable part of your golden handshake may be charged at a lower tax rate.

For the over 65s:

- Do remember that age allowance (a higher personal allowance) is available for those aged 65, and for those over 75 there is a higher-age allowance available.

The self-employed

The self-employed have considerably more flexibility in their tax saving arrangements than employees, and those who are self-employed are probably well aware of the sort of advantages they may legitimately take. However, here are two that should not be overlooked:

1. If you are starting in business and need to draw all your profit to fund your living expenses, it may not be advisable to form a limited company straight away, even though there are tax savings to be made. As a self-employed trader, you have more flexibility and lower administrative costs. You can always incorporate later.

2. A pension scheme is a most efficient way of diverting surplus profits into a tax-free lump sum and pension for the future.

Claimable expenses for the self-employed

Basic costs and general running expenses

Normally allowed – The cost of goods bought for resale and raw materials used in business. Advertising, delivery charges, heating, lighting, cleaning, rates, telephone. The rent of business premises. The replacement of small tools and special clothing. Postage, stationery, relevant books and magazines. Accountants' fees. Bank charges on business accounts. Fees to professional bodies. Security expenditure.

Not allowed – The initial cost of machinery, vehicles, equipment, permanent advertising signs – but you can claim capital allowances. The cost of buildings. Providing for anticipated expenses in the future.

Use of home for work

Normally allowed – The business proportion of telephone, lighting, heating, cleaning, insurance. The business proportion of rent and Council Tax. If you use part of your home exclusively for business, claiming these costs may mean some Capital Gains Tax to pay if you sell your home – but this is unlikely.

Wages and salaries

Normally allowed – Wages, salaries, redundancy and leaving payments paid to employees. Pensions for past employees and their dependants. Staff training. Reasonable pay for your spouse, provided that they are actually employed.

Not allowed – Your own wages or salary or that of any business partner. Your own drawings.

Tax and National Insurance

Normally allowed – Employer's National Insurance contributions for employees.

Not allowed – Income Tax. Capital Gains Tax. Inheritance Tax. Your own National Insurance contributions.

Entertaining

Normally allowed – Entertainment of own staff (e.g. a Christmas party).

Not allowed – Any other business entertaining.

Pre-trading

Normally allowed – Revenue business expenditure incurred within five years before starting to trade.

Gifts

Normally allowed – Gifts costing up to £50 a year to each person so long as the gift advertises your business (or things it sells). Gifts (whatever their value) to employees.

Not allowed – Food, drink, tobacco or vouchers for goods given to anyone other than employees.

Travelling

Normally allowed – Hotel and travelling expenses on business trips. Travel between different places of work. The running costs of your own car – whole of cost if used wholly for business, proportion if used privately too.

Not allowed – Travel between home and business. The cost of buying a car or van (but you can claim capital allowances).

If a business leases a car costing more than £12,000, part of the leasing cost is disallowed for tax purposes. The rules are complicated, but, in principle, the more expensive the car you lease, the smaller the proportion that you will be allowed to claim as a tax deduction in your accounts.

Interest payments

Normally allowed – The interest on overdrafts and loans for business purposes.

Not allowed – The interest on capital paid or credited to partners.

Hire purchase

Normally allowed – Hire charge part of instalments (i.e. the amount you pay less the cash price).

Not allowed – Cash price of what you are buying on hire purchase (but you may get capital allowances).

Hiring

Normally allowed – Reasonable charge for hire of capital goods, including cars.

Insurance

Normally allowed – Business insurance (e.g. employer's liability, fire and theft, motor, insuring employees' lives).

Not allowed – Your own life insurance.

Trade marks

Normally allowed – Fees paid to register a trademark, design or patent.

Not allowed – The cost of buying a patent from someone else (but you may get capital allowances).

Legal costs

Normally allowed – The costs of recovering debts, defending business rights, preparing service agreements, appealing against rates, renewing a lease for a period not exceeding 50 years (but not if a premium is paid).

Not allowed – Expenses (including stamp duty) for acquiring land, buildings or leases. Fines and other penalties for breaking the law.

Repairs

Normally allowed – Normal repairs and maintenance to premises or equipment.

Not allowed – The cost of additions, alterations, improvements (but you may get capital allowances).

Debts

Normally allowed – Specific provisions for debts and debts written off.

Not allowed – General reserve for bad or doubtful debts.

Subscriptions

Normally allowed – Payments which secure benefits for your business or staff. Payments to societies that have arrangements with HMRC (in some cases only a proportion). However, do watch for possible National Insurance contributions.

Not allowed – Payments to political parties, churches and charities (but small gifts to charities may be allowed if there is a local advertising motive).

Personal taxpayers, both rich and poor

Higher-rate taxpayers

For those with high income (i.e. into the 40 per cent tax band), and particularly if surplus to requirements, funds can be diverted to the following havens for tax advantages either on initial payment or at a later date:

- **Life assurance:** investing in a 'with profits' endowment policy that will run for at least ten years can produce a good tax-free return.

- **National Savings Certificates:** these can produce a good tax-free income. It's always a good idea to keep aware of what National Savings Schemes have on offer.

- **Perks in quoted shares:** many quoted shares now offer perks to their shareholders and these are entirely tax free.

- **National Insurance:** if you have more than one source of employment earnings and you are in danger of paying more than the maximum, why not defer Class 1 contributions on one of the employments to avoid making an overpayment?

- **Investments** in:

1. pensions;

2. the Enterprise Investment Scheme (EIS);

   You can invest up to £500,000 in Enterprise Investment Scheme (EIS) shares and you will get Income Tax relief of 20 per cent on that amount. When you sell, you get full Capital Gains Tax relief. There is a minimum investment of £500.

   Half of an investment made before 6 October may be carried back to the previous tax year for Income Tax purposes (up to a maximum of £50,000).

   You must hold your Enterprise Investment Scheme shares for at least three years or the relief will be withdrawn (five years in the case of shares issued before 6 April 2000).

   Any loss you make on the sale of the shares is available against either capital gains or income.

   You must not be connected with the company (i.e. hold over 30 per cent of the shares or be an employee), although you can become a director of the company and still qualify for EIS relief as long as you were not connected with the company before the shares were issued.

   Deferral relief: in addition to the above, if you have made a capital gain this year, and if you reinvest all that gain in the purchase of EIS shares, you can thereby defer all the Capital Gains Tax payable this year on that gain until you sell your EIS shares.

3. a Venture Capital Trust (see page 13);

4. unquoted shares.

For low earners

Young earners

Young people starting in employment have little scope for tax saving (usually because they have a low income), but they should not overlook the favourable Capital Gains Tax treatment available for those who purchase their main residence. Very few people have ever regretted buying their own home.

Other low earners

Don't forget that if you are a low earner, whether in employment or self-employment, you may be able to avoid either Class 1 or Class 2 National Insurance contributions. You should not claim exemption from Class 2 contributions on the basis of low earnings unless you are already paying contributions on another source of income. If you don't pay, you build up no entitlement to benefits or pension rights. £2.30 per week is a small sum to pay to safeguard this entitlement.

 Children

Surplus after-tax income transferred by parents to their children is usually non-taxable in the hands of the child. However, where children earn income exceeding £100 in any tax year on capital provided by their parents, the whole income will be counted as that of their parents.

Make sure that savings accounts with building societies or banks in children's names are paying interest gross. Ask the bank for, and complete, Form R85, which certifies the children as non-taxpayers.

100 Capital Gains Tax planning

- **Married couples:** each spouse will be taxed on their own gains and will receive a non-transferable annual exemption of £9,600.

- **Annual exemptions:** do remember to maximise them. To this end you could delay disposals until after the next 5 April if you have already used your current exemption or, alternatively, bring forward planned disposals to before 6 April if you have not yet used your exemption, or split the disposals of an asset, such as blocks of shares, to straddle 5 April in order to obtain the benefit of two years' exemptions. Consider whether you can wait until after 5 April to make the sales so as to delay the tax payment by a further 12 months.

- **Assets of negligible value:** if you hold an asset (e.g. shares in a company) which has lost most of its value, you may be able to claim the capital loss now against your capital gains. Ask your tax inspector if they will allow the loss.

- **Loans and guarantees:** you may obtain relief for losses on loans and guarantees made to people who have used the money wholly for the purpose of their business. Relief is not available if the loss or guarantee arises through your own act or omission or where the borrower is your husband or wife.

- **Gifts:** all gifts are exempt from stamp duty.

- **Gifts between spouses:** no capital gain or loss arises on gifts between husband and wife, but the recipient takes over the other spouse's acquisition date and original value.

- **Gifts to charities:** because these are exempt from Capital Gains Tax it's often better, if you intend making a charitable donation of an asset which would realise a gain on disposal (e.g. shares), to consider donating the asset rather than the equivalent amount of cash. The charity may subsequently sell the shares and realise the gain free of tax because of its privileged status.

- **Holdover relief for gifts:** this is restricted to business assets, heritage property and property on which there is an immediate charge to Inheritance Tax. Don't always claim holdover relief – it's sometimes cheaper to pay a small amount of tax than to hold over the tax bill of some considerably greater sum to the future.

- **Assets to children:** if you have assets which you expect will increase in value over a period of time, consider giving them to your children now.

- **Main residence:** no Capital Gains Tax is payable on the disposal of your home. Taking in a lodger doesn't affect your main residence relief but letting the property may.

101 Inheritance Tax planning

- Married couples and civil partners should remember the doubling up of the nil-rate band. From 9 October 2007, each couple has a joint tax-free band of £624,000 (for 2008/09), which is to increase to £700,000 in 2010–2011.

- It's now possible to give away £312,000 every seven years without a charge to Inheritance Tax arising. However, there may be Capital Gains Tax on a non-cash gift, so take professional advice.

- There is tapering relief on gifts so that, as the years up to seven slip by, the tax bill does reduce significantly.

- It's important to remember, in planning to reduce the Inheritance Tax bill upon your death, not to give away too much unless you can genuinely afford to do so. If you wish to make a gift of your family home but also wish to continue living in it, you must either pay full market rent for the privilege or consult a specialist Inheritance Tax adviser who can provide a sophisticated planning scheme to circumvent the 'reservation of benefit' rules. With no Capital Gains Tax arising on death it's sometimes better to let properties pass on death rather than before. However, this matter must be carefully weighed up before a decision is made.

- Lifetime gifts: gifts between husband and wife are exempt from Inheritance Tax.

- Remember, you can give away the annual Inheritance-Tax-free exempt sum of £3,000, which may be doubled up if it wasn't used in the previous year.

- Gifts of up to £250 per year to an individual are tax free.

- Gifts out of surplus income are tax free; take professional advice on this.

- Wedding gifts up to certain limits are tax free.

- Term assurance is a sensible means of protecting a gift that has been made should tax become due as a result of death within seven years.

- Always make a Will and build the necessary tax planning points into it. Discuss this with your solicitor.

- Special reliefs: generally, business assets attract some measure of relief, as does woodland and agricultural property. Agricultural property without a right to vacant possession may attract a smaller relief.

- Trusts for younger children: this is a complicated subject and advice must be sought from your solicitor.

- Doubling up the main residence relief: it doesn't make good sense for you to buy a house or flat for your adult children to live in since any gain you make on its subsequent sale will be chargeable to Capital Gains Tax. Instead, consider providing your child with the necessary funds to make the purchase in their own name and you could do this by making an interest-free loan which you reduce each year by the annual £3,000 exemption.

- Incorporation of a growing business: it may be advantageous to give shares in the company to your children and/or grandchildren soon after incorporation when their value is relatively low.

Appendix

Tax rates and allowances for 2008/09

Income Tax		Taxable Income		
	Band	From	To	Rate
Basic Rate		0	34,800	20%
Higher Rate		34,801		40%

Capital Gains Tax (for individuals)	First	9,600	Exempt

New single rate of 18% plus new entrepreneurs' relief

Corporation Tax	Band	From	To	Rate
Small Companies Rate		1	300,000	21%
Marginal Relief		300,001	1,500,000	29.75%
Main Rate		1,500,000		28%

Inheritance Tax (on death)	Band	From	To	Rate
Nil Rate Band		0	312,000	0%
Over Nil Rate Band		312,000		40%

Personal Allowances
Personal 6,035
Personal (aged 65 to 74) 9,030
Married Couples (aged less than 75)*# 6,535
Personal (aged over 75) 9,180
Married Couples (aged over 75)*# 6,625

All 2 higher age allowances are only available for incomes up to £21,800 in 2008/09
* = relief restricted to 10%   # = husband or wife must be born before 6 April 1935

National Insurance
Class 1 (Employment) Earnings per week

Employee (not contracted out)
Up to £105 Nil
£105 to £770 11%
Over £770 1%
Employer (not contracted out)
Up to £105 Nil
Over £105 12.8%

Class 2 (Self-Employment) (The old weekly stamp) £2.30
No contributions due if profits below £4,825

Class 4 (Self-Employment) 8% on profits between £5,435 and £40,040

1% on profits over £40,040

State Pension		Week	Year
Single		90.70	£4,716.40
Married		145.05	£7,542.60
Age addition (over 80)		0.25	£13.00

VAT Threshold with effect from 1 April £67,000
Rate 17.5%

Stamp Duty	From/to	0	150,000	Nil
	From/to	150,001	250,000	1%
	From/to	250,001	500,000	3%
	From/to	500,000		4%

Taxable Car Benefits *Fuel Benefit* As with Car Benefit, the taxable charge is based on CO_2 emissions. The charge is based on a sum of £16,900 for all cars, not on the price of the car.

Car Benefit The scale charge is based on CO_2 emissions. The Annual Charge ranges from 10% for eco-friendly cars to 35% for Gas Guzzlers. Alternative rates apply to cars registered before 1.1.1998. Diesels attract a 3% surcharge, but not over 35% and not if they are Euro 4 compliant and registered before 6.4.06.

Van Benefit
Van Scale Charge £3,000
Fuel Scale Charge for Vans £500

Car Mileage Allowance All Engine Sizes
Up to 10,000 miles pa 40p
Over 10,000 miles pa 25p

Tax rates and allowances for 2007/08

Income Tax

	Band	Taxable Income From	To	Rate
Starting Rate		0	2,230	10%
Basic Rate		2,231	34,600	22%
Higher Rate		34,601		40%

Capital Gains Tax (for individuals)

		First	9,200	Exempt
Balance taxed at 20% and/or 40%				
Taper relief for long-term gains				

Corporation Tax

	Band	From	To	Rate
Small Companies Rate		1	300,000	20%
Marginal Relief		300,001	1,500,000	32.5%
Main Rate		1,500,000		30%

Inheritance Tax (on death)

	Band	From	To	Rate
Nil Rate Band		0	300,000	0%
Over Nil Rate Band		300,000		40%

Personal Allowances

Personal	5,225
Personal (aged 65 to 74)	7,550
Married Couples (aged 65 to 74)*#	6,285
Personal (aged over 75)	7,690
Married Couples (aged over 75)*#	6,365

All 2 higher age allowances are only available for incomes up to £20,900 in 2007/08
* = relief restricted to 10%   # = husband or wife must be born before 6 April 1935

National Insurance
Class 1 (Employment)   Earnings per week

Employee (not contracted out)	
Up to £100	Nil
£100 to £670	11%
Over £670	1%
Employer (not contracted out)	
Up to £100	Nil
Over £100	12.8%

Class 2 (Self-Employment) (The old weekly stamp) — £2.20
No contributions due if profits below £4,635

Class 4 (Self-Employment) 8% on profits between £5,225 and £34,840

1% on profits over £34,840

State Pension

	Week	Year
Single	87.30	£4,539.60
Married	139.60	£7,259.20
Age addition (over 80)	0.25	£13.00

VAT

Threshold with effect from 1 April	£64,000
Rate	17.5%

Stamp Duty

From/to	0	125,000	Nil
From/to	125,001	250,000	1%
From/to	250,001	500,000	3%
From/to	500,000		4%

Taxable Car Benefits

Fuel Benefit — As with Car Benefit, the taxable charge is based on CO_2 emissions. The charge is based on a sum of £14,400 for all cars, not on the price of the car.

Car Benefit — The scale charge is based on CO_2 emissions. The Annual Charge ranges from 15% for eco-friendly cars to 35% for Gas Guzzlers. There is no adjustment for the age of the car, nor for business mileage driven. Alternative rates apply to cars registered before 1.1.1998. Diesels attract a 3% surcharge, but not over 35% and not if they are Euro 4 compliant and registered before 6.4.06.

Van Benefit — Any Age of Vehicle

Van Scale Charge	£3,000
Fuel Scale Charge for Vans	£500

Car Mileage Allowance — All Engine Sizes

Up to 10,000 miles pa	40p
Over 10,000 miles pa	25p

VAT fuel scale charges for three-month periods

CO_2 band, g/km	VAT fuel scale charge, three-month period £	VAT on three-month charge £	VAT exclusive three-month charge £
120 or less	138.00	20.55	117.45
125	207.00	30.83	176.17
130	207.00	30.83	176.17
135	207.00	30.83	176.17
140	221.00	32.91	188.09
145	234.00	34.85	199.15
150	248.00	36.94	211.06
155	262.00	39.02	222.98
160	276.00	41.11	234.89
165	290.00	43.19	246.81
170	303.00	45.13	257.87
175	317.00	47.21	269.79
180	331.00	49.30	281.70
185	345.00	51.38	293.62
190	359.00	53.47	305.53
195	373.00	55.55	317.45
200	386.00	57.49	328.51
205	400.00	59.57	340.43
210	414.00	61.66	352.34
215	428.00	63.74	364.26
220	442.00	65.83	376.17
225	455.00	67.77	387.23
230	469.00	69.85	399.15
235 or more	483.00	71.94	411.06

Index